Oral Arguments and Coalition Formation on the U.S. Supreme Court

The U.S. Supreme Court, with its controlled, highly institutionalized decision-making practices, provides an ideal environment for studying coalition formation. The process begins during the oral argument stage, which provides the justices with their first opportunity to hear one another's attitudes and concerns specific to a case, information that eventually allows them to form a coalition. To uncover the workings of this process, the authors analyze the oral argument transcripts from every case decided from 1998 through 2007 as well as the complete collection of notes kept during oral arguments by Justices Lewis F. Powell (1972–87) and Harry A. Blackmun (1970–94). The book illuminates a key aspect of the Court's decision-making process and represents a major step forward in the understanding of coalition formation, which is crucial for many areas of political debate and decision making.

Ryan C. Black is Assistant Professor of Political Science at Michigan State University.

Timothy R. Johnson is Morse Alumni Distinguished Teaching Professor of Political Science at the University of Minnesota.

Justin Wedeking is Assistant Professor of Political Science at the University of Kentucky.

Oral Arguments and Coalition Formation on the U.S. Supreme Court: A Deliberate Dialogue

Ryan C. Black, Timothy R. Johnson, and Justin Wedeking

THE UNIVERSITY OF MICHIGAN PRESS

Ann Arbor

Published in the United States of America by
The University of Michigan Press
Manufactured in the United States of America
♾ Printed on acid-free paper

2015 2014 2013 2012 4 3 2 1

A CIP catalog record for this book is available from the British Library.

Library of Congress Cataloging-in-Publication Data

Black, Ryan C., 1982–
Oral arguments and coalition formation on the U.S. Supreme Court : a deliberate dialogue / Ryan C. Black, Timothy R. Johnson, and Justin Wedeking.
p. cm.
Includes bibliographical references and index.
ISBN 978-0-472-11846-5 (cloth : alk. paper) — ISBN 978-0-472-02865-8 (e-book)
1. United States. Supreme Court—Decision making. 2. Oral pleading—United States. 3. Judicial process—United States. 4. Forensic orations—United States. I. Johnson, Timothy R. II. Wedeking, Justin. III. Title.
KF8742.B57 2012
347.73'265—dc23

2012012804

For Bailey and Hunter—RCB

For my early morning hoops companions—TRJ

For Lauren and Megan—JW

Contents

Acknowledgments

This book could not have been written without the help of many people. First, we thank Melody Herr and the staff at the University of Michigan Press. Melody's guidance as an editor has been first-rate, and we could not have completed this project without her excellent help. We also greatly appreciate Kevin Rennells for guiding us through the editing process.

During the research and writing process, many people provided us with great assistance and insight. We thank Amanda Bryan, Caitlin Dwyer, Dan Thaler, and Sarah Treul for their able research assistance. For reading drafts and for giving advice on substance and methods, we thank Amanda Bryan, Paul Goren, Tom Hammond, Joanne Miller, Ryan Owens, Jason Roberts, Maron Sorenson, Jim Spriggs, Jeff Staton, Paul Wahlbeck, and the participants at the University of Kentucky Law School's Brown Bag Workshop. We thank the Blackmun estate and the staff of the Manuscript Reading Room at the Library of Congress for their help with the Blackmun files; we thank the Powell estate and Washington and Lee University, along with John Jacob, for excellent assistance in using the Powell archives. For converting our original manuscript, copyediting, and being an all-around rock star, we thank Maron Sorenson. Naturally, all errors remain ours.

Black thanks his colleagues and Michigan State University for their ongoing support of his research. He thanks Krista, his wife, for her patience and support, both of which he undoubtedly tested while working on this book.

Johnson thanks his colleagues for providing support and the University of Minnesota for a single-semester leave so that he had time to work on the manuscript. He also thanks his wife, Julie, and his boys, Alexi, Aidan, and Satchel, for ensuring he always knows what is most important in life.

Wedeking thanks his colleagues for providing support and the University of Kentucky for providing time and resources to work on the manuscript. He also thanks his wife, Michelle, for her continued support. He dedicates the book to his two daughters, Lauren and Megan.

Finally, we gratefully acknowledge the National Science Foundation for its generous financial support of our collaborative work on gathering, digitizing, and disseminating Supreme Court arguments on the Web (IIS-0324992 and IIS-0325282).

The authors' names appear alphabetically.

A Note to the Reader

Oral Arguments and Coalition Formation on the U.S. Supreme Court offers insights into the Supreme Court's decision-making process and utilizes a wide range of data to demonstrate how the oral argument phase of this process affects the justices' decisions. To that end, we provide extensive anecdotes of specific exchanges between Court and counsel. While we quote extensively from these exchanges, we also bring them to life for the reader; where we quote from a transcript, we provide notes that link the specific exchanges to audio files at the University of Michigan Press's website: http://www.press.umich.edu/titleDetailDesc.do?id=4599894. In addition, several of the figures showing the handwritten notes of Justices Blackmun and Powell can be found in color at this link. We hope that you enjoy this aspect of the book and that it helps provide a better understanding of the inner workings of our nation's highest court.

1 | Introduction

On June 25, 2009, the U.S. Supreme Court decided *Horne v. Flores.* The case focused on whether the state of Arizona took appropriate action to overcome barriers to English-language learning in its schools and whether Arizona's compliance with the language requirements of the No Child Left Behind Act of 2001 was consistent with the "appropriate action" standard required by the Equal Education Opportunity Act of 1974. The Court's decision is certainly important for its impact on national educational policy. It is also important for another, less obvious, reason—the justices' behavior and interactions with one another during the oral arguments two months prior to the public announcement of their final decision. Indeed, the majority and dissenting coalitions that ultimately formed in June originated in how the justices dealt with one another during these proceedings. To see how, we turn back the clock to April 20, 2009.

The oral argument began with the customary opening statement made by all advocates: "Mr. Chief Justice, and may it please the Court"; but that was the extent to which the petitioner's attorney stayed on script (oral argument transcript, 2). This development probably surprised those in the gallery that day because standing at the lectern was not a legal lightweight appearing before the Court for the first time; rather, it was former solicitor general Kenneth Starr, representing Arizona and superintendent Tom Horne. Despite his prominence, Starr completed exactly one sentence about the history of the case before Justice David Souter interrupted with a question about the lower court's precise determination. Starr responded briefly, but with the session still barely a minute old, Souter launched into a lengthy second question that ended with him inquiring, "Am I—am I wrong on [what the lower court determination was]?" (oral argument transcript, 2). Starr, perhaps channeling Ed McMahon, responded with "You are correct" (oral argument transcript, 2).

Having ostensibly satisfied Souter, Starr tried to move on but was interrupted several more times. These interruptions made it difficult for him to press his next point—that the school district in question was improving and was doing "great." Starr battled to keep his argument on track while the justices raised questions that piqued their interest and that, as former solicitor general Theodore Olson once put it, enabled them to "make points to their colleagues" (Biskupic 2006).

Just when Starr seemed to have an opportunity to hammer home his argument, he was interrupted again, this time by Justice Stephen Breyer. Breyer challenged Starr's assessment of progress in Arizona by citing a list of statistics that suggested that the program's objectives had yet to be achieved. At this point, Starr was not even in a position to add much to the discussion. In fact, as Justice Antonin Scalia entered the conversation, it was uncertain when Starr would have a chance to speak. In particular, Scalia was confused about the statistics Breyer referenced. When Starr could not immediately clarify the matter, Scalia said, "If you can't answer that, I think Justice Breyer can. But I would like to know what comparison—" (oral argument transcript, 5). Breyer continued with the interruptions, saying, "He doesn't actually have the right to ask me questions." Scalia then replied, "I don't. That's—that's exactly true. But—." To calm the atmosphere, Chief Justice John Roberts spoke up: "Very much true. Counsel, why don't you try to answer?" (oral argument transcript, 5).

Although Starr tried to highlight data found in an appendix to his brief, Roberts prodded him to refine and reshape his response: "Well, I still don't have an answer to Justice Breyer's—I guess Justice Scalia's question following up on Justice Breyer's. What are the parameters or the—data with respect to the figures Justice Breyer gave you?" Again, Starr did not provide the exact answer Roberts sought, so the Chief Justice tried another tack: "So the answer is that Justice Breyer's figures are correct with respect to the appropriate bases of children. You are just saying that you want to use a different test than the one that he was quoting?" When Starr refused to confirm what appeared to be a helpful point, Roberts tried a third angle: "The figures are accurate. You just think a different test should be used?" This time, when Starr responded, Breyer interrupted to press Starr on what test he preferred.

While the argument moved on to address other issues, ideological cleavages among the Court's members were readily apparent (Lowy 2009). They also turned out to be persistent. Just over two months later, the Court decided *Horne* by a 5-4 vote. After going head-to-head during oral arguments, Breyer and Scalia now faced off in opposing coalitions, with Scalia joining a majority opinion authored by Justice Samuel Alito. Breyer wrote the Court's dissenting opinion. Oral argument portended not just the vote outcome in the case but also the argumentative basis for the opinions issued by the competing coalitions.

Consider first the majority opinion. Among other arguments, Alito's opinion remanded the case for "further factual findings regarding whether [the] implementation of the policy in question was a 'changed circumstance' warranting relief" (23–25). In other words, the majority argued that the district court must reconsider the factual record—as discussed at oral argument—on four separate issues. Breyer's dissent also moved directly to a point he raised during oral argument—the flaw in the school district's factual determination would have adverse effects on students. As he put it, "I fear that the Court misapplies an inappropriate procedural framework, reaching a result that neither the record nor the law adequately supports. In doing so, it risks denying schoolchildren the English-learning instruction necessary 'to overcome language barriers that impede' their 'equal participation.'" In sum, for both the majority and the dissent, the questions raised by Scalia, Roberts, and Breyer during oral argument corresponded with both coalition composition and the specific policy content articulated by the two sides.

This book addresses one of the most important questions social scientists have sought to answer: How and why do coalitions form when groups make decisions? We focus on the process of coalition formation on the U.S. Supreme Court. Specifically, we suggest that the sequence of events in *Horne* is neither anomalous nor limited to recent Court decisions. Instead, it is indicative of how justices interact in almost every case they decide. That is, they interrupt one another, listen to what others have to say, and ultimately try to use what they learn from these interactions to determine how they will decide the legal and policy issues before them. Generally, then, we contend that oral arguments mark the beginning of what can be both a contentious and long process of building a majority coalition on the U.S. Supreme Court.

In so doing, we make several contributions to our understanding of coalition formation and Supreme Court decision making. First, we provide a novel theoretical perspective that crosses disciplinary boundaries to link the literature on coalition formation with insights from social psychology. Doing so allows us to analyze how political decision makers interact with one another. Second, we draw on a unique mixture of archival and contemporary data—much of it new to the literature—to demonstrate how justices gather and then use information from oral arguments to help them make coalitions. Third, and most specifically, we make a key contribution to the growing literature that focuses on how Supreme Court oral arguments affect the decisions justices make.

Our decision to focus on the Supreme Court is a deliberate one, reached after a careful consideration of the unique benefits of analyzing its inner workings. The Court provides a particularly good environment for analyzing coalition formation because of the controlled and highly institutionalized nature of its decision-making process. That is, because the institutional structure is constant (even over time), we have an unparalleled opportunity to uncover how the justices' interactions with one another affect who joins a majority coalition when cases are decided.

At the same time, we also believe that this book offers important insights beyond the Supreme Court. Coalition formation has broad importance for political scientists and others. Indeed, interest in coalition formation crosses disciplinary boundaries and is important to fields as diverse as sociology (e.g., Strodtbeck 1954; Gamson 1961), economics (von Neumann and Morgenstern 1953), and psychology (Kahan and Rapoport 1984). More specifically, the study of coalitions ties directly into some of the most fundamental questions of politics and political science. With only a handful of exceptions, our government is premised on the concept of majority rule. Hence, to understand what resources and rights are allocated to which groups and interests at what times, any analysis must begin by examining how majorities form or dissolve. We, of course, are not the first to make this observation. Easton (1953), for example, defines politics as the authoritative allocation of values. Among his many contributions to the field, Riker (1962, 12) offers a refinement of this notion when he argues that "much the greater part of the study of the authoritative allocation of values is reduced to the study of coalitions."

Our argument offers a step forward for political scientists' understanding of coalition formation among political actors. Indeed, the insights we provide can be translated to the process through which members of Congress and bureaucrats use hearings to gather information before they make decisions. Thus, we believe that although our analysis concerns one particular institution, our theoretical argument is broad based and will be useful to many areas of political science.[1]

The remainder of this chapter has several goals. We begin by fleshing out our initial claim that oral arguments, as a general matter, are an important part of the Court's decision-making process to which scholars, advocates, and justices alike should pay attention. Second, we provide some facial support for this theory by turning to statements from justices, attorneys, and Court watchers. Third, we offer a theoretical account that links components of coalition formation to Supreme Court oral arguments. Finally, we summarize our plan for the remainder of the book.

The Importance of Oral Arguments

The justices' behavior during oral arguments in *Horne* highlights a point that has, until recently, been less than obvious to legal scholars and political scientists alike: These proceedings can play a key role in the Court's decision-making process. Many students of the Court think otherwise. For example, Rohde and Spaeth (1976) assert that oral arguments have little influence on the outcome of a case because justices' voting preferences are stable. More specifically, Rohde and Spaeth posit that while "oral argument frequently provides an indication of which is the most likely basis for decision," it "does not . . . provide reliable clues as to how a given justice may vote" (153). Segal and Spaeth (2002, 280) concur, contending that there is no indication that oral argument "regularly, or even frequently, determines who wins and who loses."

As further evidence that justices do not think about these proceedings as they decide the legal and policy issues of a case, Segal and Spaeth (2002, 280) point out that Justice Lewis Powell's copious conference notes make almost no references to oral argument. Segal and Spaeth suggest that because conference (where justices cast initial votes in a case) occurs within a day or so of oral argument and because none of the justices used the words *oral argument* during private conference discussions, the proceedings in open court must not affect the outcome of the case.[2] Generally, then, for Rohde and Spaeth and Segal and Spaeth, justices' votes will not change as a result of what transpires during a one-hour exchange between Court and counsel.

The idea that oral arguments have little bearing on case outcomes stems from the prevalence of the attitudinal model, which posits that justices simply vote for their preferred outcome and are not influenced by external factors including the law or their colleagues' preferences (Segal and Spaeth 2002). Despite this claim, the preponderance of evidence emanating from political science (e.g., Epstein and Knight 1998; Maltzman, Spriggs, and Wahlbeck 2000; Hammond, Bonneau, and Sheehan 2005) and legal scholarship (e.g., Harvey and Friedman 2006) demonstrates that the various points of the decision-making process can and do affect case outcomes. Indeed, scholars have shown that agenda setting (Black and Owens 2009), the order of voting at conference (Johnson, Spriggs, and

Wahlbeck 2005), opinion assignment (Maltzman and Wahlbeck 2004), and bargaining over opinion content (Spriggs, Maltzman, and Wahlbeck 1999; Maltzman, Spriggs, and Wahlbeck 2000) influence the choices justices make.

In the midst of the Court's decision-making process, justices sit with one another to hear oral arguments from attorneys representing both sides of a dispute. Evidence establishes that these proceedings generally play an integral role in the Court's decision-making process (Johnson 2004; Wrightsman 2008). More specifically, this one-hour conversation between Court and counsel as well as among the justices themselves connects with the outcome of a case in myriad ways. Justices, for example, use these proceedings to gather additional information not contained in the litigants' briefs (Wasby, D'Amato, and Metrailer 1977; Johnson 2004). Such information includes the facts of the case, pertinent precedent, and how Congress or the president might respond if the Court decides in a particular way.

In addition, evidence indicates that the quality of arguments forwarded by attorneys during these proceedings affects justices' votes (Johnson, Wahlbeck, and Spriggs 2006). Indeed, even justices predisposed to vote for a particular side (based on their ideological predilections) tend to vote more often for the side that offers better arguments in open court. Finally, mounting evidence suggests that during oral arguments, justices foreshadow how they will decide (Shullman 2004; Roberts 2005; Johnson et al. 2009; Black et al. 2011). Such signals emanate from the number of questions justices ask the attorney for each side of the dispute as well as from the emotive tenor of these questions. When justices give one side a harder time (by asking more questions) or when they ask that side questions using less pleasant language, that side is more likely to lose the case.

Oral Argument as a Conversation among Justices

While this argument may be intuitive in its application to the Court, it is not clear whether the justices use oral arguments as a forum to help them build majority (and possibly dissenting) coalitions. Some evidence certainly suggests that they begin the coalition-building process during these proceedings (see, e.g., Wasby, D'Amato, and Metrailer 1976; Johnson 2004; Johnson, Spriggs, and Wahlbeck 2007), but most of these findings are based on a single justice's behavior, on a small number of cases, or on anecdotal accounts. We do know, however, that justices, attorneys, and keen Court watchers have pegged oral arguments as an important (and possibly the only) forum in which justices hold full-fledged conversations with one another about cases they have chosen to decide. In fact, each of these groups posits that the justices utilize these proceedings to learn about their colleagues' preferences and to make legal or policy points to one another, not simply to ask questions of the attorneys.

The View from the Bench

We begin with the justices' contention that oral arguments launch the process through which coalitions form as the justices work their way toward a final majority opinion on the merits. According to Justice Anthony Kennedy, he and his colleagues almost never discuss cases prior to these proceedings. In fact, the norm among the justices is that they should not have such discussions.[3] As he puts it, "Before the case is heard, we have an unwritten rule: We don't talk about it with each other. . . . If the rule is violated, we send a memo to everybody about what we've talked about, because we don't want little cliques or cabals or little groups that lobby each other before" (Liptak 2010). Roberts echoes this sentiment in describing the role of oral arguments:

> It's the first time we learn what our colleagues think about a case. We don't sit down before argument and say, "This is what we think" or "This is how I view the case." We come to it cold as far as knowing what everybody thinks, and so through the questioning, we're learning for the first time what the other justices view and how they view the case, and that can alter how you view it right on the spot. And if they're raising questions about an issue that you hadn't thought was important, you can start looking into that issue during the questioning a little bit. (C-SPAN 2009)

The justices seem to want to ensure the integrity of their decision-making process and therefore wait until the point at which they appear in open court to begin the process of persuading one another about how to decide a case. Kennedy confirms this assessment of the process: "The first time we know what our colleagues are thinking is in oral arguments from the questions" (Liptak 2010). Kennedy previously explained, "When the people come . . . to see our arguments, they often see a dialogue between the justices asking a question and the attorney answering it. And they think of the argument as a series of these dialogues. It isn't that. As John

[Paul Stevens] points out, what is happening is the court is having a conversation with itself through the intermediary of the attorney" (qtd. in O'Brien 2000, 260). Roberts's and Kennedy's views of how justices utilize these proceedings support our intuition about the coalition-formation process beginning at oral arguments.

We also find support for the idea these face-to-face conversations are important to the justices. Indeed, many of Kennedy's colleagues make clear they are, by and large, engaging in conversations with one another during oral arguments. As we learn from the exchange among Breyer, Roberts, and Scalia in *Horne,* however, the justices do not always do so by speaking directly to one another on the bench, since such actions also would violate Court norms. As Greenhouse (1989) explains, "Court protocol does not permit justices to address one another directly from the bench, so, as often happens when justices want to do so anyway, the debate between the two was conducted through questions that each posed."

Other justices share Roberts's and Kennedy's view that oral arguments are largely a conversation among the justices. Even Scalia, who once publicly suggested that oral arguments were a "a dog and pony show" (qtd. in O'Brien 2000, 260) realizes that oral argument "isn't just an interchange between counsel and each of the individual justices: What is going on is to some extent an exchange of information among justices themselves" (PBS 1988). When attorneys present their arguments, they must account for this fact. As former Chief Justice William Rehnquist (2001, 244) posits, "The judges' questions, although nominally directed to the attorney arguing the case, may in fact be for the benefit of their colleagues. A good advocate will recognize this fact and make use of it during his presentation." The bottom line is that justices from across the ideological spectrum believe that interactions with one another during oral arguments constitute an important part of their decision-making process.[4]

Of course, the question is whether and how such interactions affect how the justices decide cases. As to the former query, Rehnquist (2001, 243) opined that "in a significant minority of cases in which I have heard oral argument, I have left the bench feeling different about the case than I did when I came on the bench. The change is seldom a full one-hundred-and-eighty-degree swing." This possible movement suggests that the interactions among justices may be key to how coalitions come together beginning at conference. With regard to how these proceedings may help justices coalesce, one former clerk argued that they may simply help colleagues to see cases slightly differently: "It's finding common ground. It was substantive. It's finding ways to move them 10 degrees" (Liptak 2010).

With this common ground, coalitions form, majority opinions are crafted, and the Court ultimately sets U.S. legal policy.

The View from the (Supreme Court) Bar

Attorneys who appear before the Court certainly share the view held by many past and present justices. In fact, as Rehnquist notes, advocates must adapt to conversations in which they act only as a messenger. Olson agrees: "It's like a highly stylized Japanese theater.... The justices use questions to make points to their colleagues" (Biskupic 2006). And as the third wheel in such a production, attorneys must, as Walter Dellinger, another former solicitor general, points out, "be speaking with not only the justice who has asked the question, but the one to whom the question is actually addressed" (Biskupic 2006). This position is also supported by Shapiro (1984, 547), who notes that "during the heat of debate on an important issue, counsel may find that one or more justices are especially persistent in questioning and appear unwilling to relent. This may be the case when a Justice is making known his or her views in an emphatic manner."

Because justices gain little or nothing from making their views known to the attorneys, we can infer that they are making a point to the other justices. Burt Neuborne, who has participated in more than one hundred cases before the Court, makes this point clear: "Sometimes I think I am a post office. I think that one of the justices wants to send a message to another justice and they are essentially arguing through me" (PBS 1988). Such conversations constitute an important part of the decision-making process because the "Justices of the Supreme Court view the [oral] argument . . . as an *initial* conference convened to decide the case" (Shapiro qtd. in Garner 2009, 7).

Ironically, attorneys do not have a favorable view of this "post office" function. For example, in a popular instructional text on Supreme Court appellate advocacy, Frederick (2003, 6) warns attorneys against becoming "the ball in a ping-pong match between members of the court who disagree with one another and use counsel's answer to advance their own positions." When justices do so, attorneys become "a mere conduit for the members of the bench to speak to one another" (6). This development is viewed unfavorably because, from the attorneys' and parties' perspective, the justices lose the benefit of analyzing the case with the attorneys' synthesis. In such instances, advocates lose control over the direction of the argument and are then forced to agree or disagree with propositions put forth from the bench (Frederick 2003). In short, the justices are no longer considering the case on terms or arguments that the party involved might view favorably.

Moreover, scholars recognize that attorneys need to avoid becoming post offices and suggest that one way to avoid doing so is by "shaping the argument" despite the seemingly incessant questioning. For example, Carroll (2000, qtd. in Garner 2009, 161) notes that "judges exercise considerable control during oral argument, and it is the goal of the astute appellate practitioner to shape the argument nonetheless, through his or her answers to questions." Being persuasive during the justices' conversation is a top goal for advocates. Yet one commonly cited reason that lawyers lose control is a rigid adherence to a script or set of prepared remarks. Conversely, being flexible is commonly cited as a powerful tool in persuading justices. For example, "Flexibility in an oral argument is . . . absolutely indispensable. A fixed or prepared [oral] argument is doomed. Your argument must adjust to the questioning of the court as well as your opponent's presentation. I must warn you that, without that adaptability, your opportunity for persuasion will be a failure" (Kaufman 1978, qtd. in Garner 2009, 159). In short, attorneys (and their instructional guides) recognize that the justices are engaged in a conversation but also readily acknowledge their goal of shaping that conversation, however difficult it might be, through their answers.

The View from beyond the Bench

Court watchers concur with the assessments made by justices and attorneys. Biskupic (2006) points out that the "hour-long sessions in the ornate courtroom also offer the justices a chance to make their own case—to each other." She goes on to suggest the justices sometimes make explicit points through the attorneys. In *Garrett v. Ceballos* (2006), for example, Roberts tried to get one of the lawyers to alter her arguments when he said to her, "[W]e would have thought you might have argued that it's speech paid for by the government . . . so there's no First Amendment issue at all" (Biskupic 2006). Similarly, after observing arguments in *Danforth v. Minnesota* (2008), Denniston (2007) notes that "there were sustained moments when it appeared that the Justices were only talking among themselves, often correcting or contradicting each other." Finally, Greenhouse (1993) describes how the justices sparred with one another in *Reno v. Shaw* (1993) to the point where it was as if Rehnquist and Scalia were coaching Shaw's attorneys on how to answer questions from Stevens: "While sympathetic justices occasionally throw lawyers a hand, it is hardly common for members of the Court to assume the role of debate coaches, as Chief Justices Rehnquist and Justice Scalia did in this instance."

Scholars agree with the assessment of the press corps, but the evidence to support such a contention is at best limited. Anecdotally, Wasby, D'Amato, and Metrailer (1977, xviii) argue that "it is not surprising that the judges would use part of the oral argument time for getting across obliquely to their colleagues on the bench arguments regarding the eventual disposition of a case." Wasby, D'Amato, and Metrailer (1976, 418) conclude, "Another, less noticed function is that oral argument serves as a means of communication between judges." Missing from these analyses, however, is a holistic account backed with systematic evidence about how these conversations specifically shape the final opinion coalition.[5] Our next step, then, is to explicate the theoretical road map that guides our journey.

The Importance of Oral Arguments for Coalition Formation

Our argument begins with the widely held belief that justices are purposive actors who seek to advance their most preferred legal policy outcomes (see, e.g., Epstein and Knight 1998; Maltzman, Spriggs, and Wahlbeck 2000). To formulate their preferred policy into law, however, they must be part of the majority coalition. To increase the likelihood of joining with their colleagues to form winning coalitions, justices must equip themselves with information about their colleagues' preferences, attitudes, concerns, and questions about a particular case. Court scholars certainly have shown that justices may gather such information during the Court's agenda-setting stage (Caldeira, Wright, and Zorn 1999), at conference (Wahlbeck, Spriggs, and Maltzman 1998), and as they bargain with one another as they craft their opinions (Maltzman, Spriggs, and Wahlbeck 2000). However, these are not the only mechanisms for obtaining information about a colleague's preferences, and they may not be the best means of doing so. In fact, we believe that oral arguments are integral to the coalition-formation process. To support this claim, we offer two criteria about the general nature of coalition formation. We then explain how Supreme Court oral arguments follow these criteria.

First, initial interactions between actors vying for a particular outcome are vital because they set the stage for all later interactions among decision makers. As Gamson (1961, 375) suggests, "To predict who will join with whom in any specific instance, the model requires information on . . . the initial distribution of resources." More specifically for our purposes, Soh and Tsatsoulis (2002) argue that the initial stage of coalition formation is critical because it allows an initiating agent to determine which groups are most likely to help form a winning coalition. In particular, they posit that the "objective of the initial coalition formation is to hastily identify potential candidates and rank them accordingly to their potential utilities" (1062).

Furthermore, uncertainty about specific outcomes of a decision-making process means that actors involved in a decision will be particularly introspective (Bettenhausen and Murnighan 1985) and look to those with whom they are interacting for clues about how a decision should be made. In fact, Bettenhausen and Murnighan (1985, 353) suggest that as actors interact, they begin to "establish . . . a basis for each actor-observer's future actions." In turn, how actors view the context of the process is set by the initial interactions: "The tentative style of these initial interactions will then give way to actions that are guided by their shared understanding of the situation" (369). Scholars from across a variety of disciplines make it clear that when the process begins is the key to understanding how final coalitions develop. Indeed, because this stage is where the action begins, everything that follows is part and parcel of the initial interactions.

Second, beyond determining when coalitions begin to form, face-to-face communication is vital to understanding this process. This argument stems from a long line of psychological and economic scholarship on coalition formation. For example, Bettenhausen and Murnighan (1985) and Murnighan and Szwajkowski (1979) suggest that face-to-face interactions are the key to how people communicate and reach decisions. Bettenhausen and Murnighan (1985, 362) find that "the group's previous face-to-face interactions became the primary determinant of the outcomes we observed." Similarly, economists have acknowledged the "crucial role of face-to-face interactions" (Cowana and Jonard 2004). Specifically, diffusion of information is best accomplished through face-to-face communication (Jaffe, Tratjenberg, and Henderson 1993; Feldman 1994; Prevezer and Swann 1996). In addition—and especially relevant for coalition formation on the Court—other scholars have found that "cooperative behavior is amplified if subjects are allowed to engage in face-to-face communication" (Schlager 1995, 254). Thus, while coalitions can form through other means, such as text-based (written) discussions, ample evidence shows that direct exchange of ideas is the best way for people to determine their best coalitions.

Supreme Court oral arguments fit both aspects of this theoretical perspective. First, two of the three other parts of the Court's coalition-formation process (conference and the written bargaining process) occur after the justices sit for oral arguments. Thus, it is natural that as the justices move to decide on the merits, these proceedings begin the series of events that culminates months later with the announcement of an opinion in open court. Justices certainly are forward-looking during the agenda-setting process (Boucher and Segal 1995), but evidence to date suggests they are simply forward-thinking about votes and not about the legal and policy content of their opinions. Johnson (2004) shows, however, that justices use oral arguments to gather information not contained in briefs submitted by litigants or amici curiae. Limited evidence also indicates that justices use these proceedings to begin learning about the legal and policy issues important to their colleagues (Johnson 2004). In short, while political scientists and legal scholars focus most of their attention on the latter stages of the Court's decision-making process, evidence demonstrates that this process begins with the oral arguments. This finding, in turn, suggests that these proceedings set the stage for all subsequent bargaining and accommodation in the Court's coalition-formation process.

Beyond the fact that oral arguments provide the first opportunity for justices to communicate with one another as they begin to decide the merits of a case, it is also their longest and only full-blown face-to-face contact during a case. Such interactions mean that these proceedings are vital for how a case is ultimately decided (Robinette 1975). Moreover, while the justices communicate during conference and as they send memorandums to one another when they craft opinions (Maltzman, Spriggs, and Wahlbeck 2000), neither setting provides the justices with a forum like oral arguments for gathering information about their colleagues. Consider the last part of the process first—bargaining and accommodation as an opinion is crafted. These exchanges among the justices are completed almost entirely in writing. It is no surprise, then, that they may not be as effective as exchanges among justices in open court.

Conference discussions, like oral arguments, provide face-to-face conversations that occur during the week.[6] The problem is that conference is not necessarily the conversation its name implies. To be sure, the justices talk to one another, but as Rehnquist (2001) suggests, these proceedings are hardly conversations because they do not last long enough for the justices to discuss the nuances of every case. In fact, it is a common misconception that the coalition-formation process starts in the first conference after oral argument. As Frederick (2003, 5) notes, "[W]ord has filtered out that the conferences [under Chief Justice Rehnquist] do not produce real dialogue in the sense of the justices exchanging views." Rehnquist (2001,

258) confirms this conjecture: "[M]y years on the Court have convinced me that the true purpose of the conference discussion of argued cases is not to persuade one's colleagues through impassioned advocacy to alter their views, but instead, by hearing each justice express his own views, to determine therefrom the view of the majority of the Court." Given this perspective, only the oral arguments provide true face-to-face conversation among the justices as they seek answers to the nation's most important legal questions.

Overall, Supreme Court oral arguments certainly meet the two criteria scholars believe are essential for coalition formation to succeed. Specifically, these proceedings are the first stage in this process for the justices and therefore may determine everything that transpires thereafter. Further, the face-to-face nature of these proceedings makes them the perfect venue for justices to figure out how to build coalitions with one another. Other justices may (perhaps simultaneously) use these proceedings to weaken arguments that may be antithetical to their preferred outcomes. In either scenario, they actively seek to determine who is likely to join a coalition with them and whose arguments may need to be combated in the opinion-writing process. Thus, to understand how majorities form to set precedent in the U.S. Supreme Court, we must understand how the justices interact with one another in open court.

Outline of the Book

The evidence we provide here contributes to an understanding and conceptualization of oral arguments as a deliberate dialogue among justices, something that is important to understanding coalition formation on our nation's court of last resort. Each chapter examines a particular aspect of these proceedings and highlights how each facet can have stunning consequences on case outcomes. Moreover, each chapter builds on its predecessor by examining another element of the justices' deliberate dialogue and linking it to the broader process of coalition formation among justices.

We begin our empirical analysis in chapter 2 by focusing on instances when justices interrupt one another without the intervention of the attorney arguing a case before them. These interactions offer explicit insight into our theoretical argument about why oral arguments help justices form coalitions with one another. Indeed, because this is the first time justices discuss the merits of a case with one another, interruptions may shift the current topic of conversation away from views that may be inimical to a given justice's preferred outcome or toward a topic more helpful to how he or she would like a case to be decided. To test this argument, we use a novel corpus of data from the 1998–2007 Court terms to isolate when justices interrupt their colleagues. Examining these interruptions is a crucial part of the coalition-formation process.

Analyzing interruptions also provides a window into the Court's inner workings because it shows how justices treat their colleagues in public. Interruptions occur on average eight times per case and have distinct patterns. Justices who take opposite ideological positions are more likely to interrupt each other. Moreover, the norm of collegiality is also enforced during oral arguments and appears to constrain how often justices interrupt one another. Specifically, justices punish those who use interruptions during oral argument by interrupting these serial offenders more often.

Chapter 3 posits that if justices use oral arguments to help build winning coalitions, then they must learn something valuable about their colleagues' preferences. From this starting point, we examine the complete collection of oral argument notes of Lewis F. Powell (1972–87) and Harry A. Blackmun (1970–94) and analyze the conditions under which these justices paid attention to their colleagues' comments and questions. These notes provide an explicit measure of learning by the justices as they sat for oral arguments. Several potential learning strategies suggest to whom Blackmun and Powell were likely to listen. In particular, we identify three theories from diverse literatures that hypothesize that justices will listen to ideologically close allies, ideologically distant foes, and justices perceived as close to the median for a given case. Blackmun referenced his colleagues in approximately 57 percent of cases, while Powell referenced his colleagues in approximately 33 percent of cases. In addition, Blackmun used these proceedings to determine where his potential adversaries might come down in the case, while Powell was more prone to listen to those with whom he might join a coalition.

Next, we analyze how such colleague-specific information corresponds with the opinion-writing process by examining other justices' reactions to draft majority opinions circulated by Powell and Blackmun. That is, we examine whether gathering more information at oral argument corresponds with the coalition-formation process. More specifically, we are interested in how the information gathered at oral argument corresponds with the responses from Blackmun's and Powell's colleagues during the opinion-writing phase of the decision-making process. Blackmun and Powell exhibited a similar pattern of receiving responses from their colleagues based on the citations made to others and the total number of notes taken in a case. Once justices learn about their colleagues, they use that information, following whatever strategy best suits them, to craft opinions their colleagues are more likely to join.

Chapter 4 takes advantage of yet another valuable feature of Blackmun's private notes: his vote predictions. In a sizable number of cases, Blackmun attempted to predict the votes of his colleagues based on what transpired during oral arguments. He did so, we argue, to help create a road map of the legal and policy elements at play in a given case. We analyze both when Blackmun attempted a prediction and the conditions under which his predictions were accurate. We find a strong relationship between the frequency with which Blackmun recorded notes for a particular justice's questions at oral arguments and his attempt to predict that colleague's vote.

In chapter 5, we summarize our findings and explore the implications of conversations at oral argument for forming coalitions and for the larger study of coalition building. We close by identifying fruitful directions for future research. First, more work remains to be done on the emotional tone and cognitive elements of what is said at oral arguments. Second, while relatively little research has focused on oral arguments, even less has focused on oral arguments of courts beyond the U.S. Supreme Court. In fact, while the study of oral arguments on the U.S. Supreme Court is important for a wide variety of reasons, examining oral argument in other courts might provide additional leverage for answering questions about how particular rules (e.g., time allotted) and procedures (e.g., allowances of rebuttals) influence the quality of information produced at oral argument.

2 | Justices' Direct Interactions during Oral Arguments

In *Danforth v. Minnesota* (2008), the U.S. Supreme Court ruled that when deciding whether to apply a precedent retroactively, states may utilize broader standards than the rule set forth by the Court. While *Danforth* was not considered a major decision of the 2007 term, the policy significantly increased states' discretionary power over how to interpret and apply retroactive rules in criminal proceedings. *Danforth* is also important and interesting because it sheds light on the justices' coalition-formation process as they stake out positions by directly interacting with one another in front of the litigants, the media, the legal community, and the public in open court. Although, as we note in chapter 1, oral arguments are formally viewed as an exchange among attorneys and justices, *Danforth* demonstrates that the conversations that transpire during these proceedings are often more of a dialogue among the justices than a discussion between the Court and counsel.

In fact, the justices at times simply ignore the attorney standing at the lectern before them. This behavior was most evident late in the *Danforth* proceedings when Stephen Breyer, Antonin Scalia, and John Paul Stevens all spoke before Patrick Diamond (arguing for the state of Minnesota) uttered a single word. The exchange began with a long hypothetical posed by Breyer (including a discussion of metaphysics and the retroactivity of law). Diamond started to respond to this hypothetical question, but Breyer spoke over him and Scalia interrupted Breyer to give his own thoughts about retroactivity and metaphysics. From there, Stevens responded to Scalia, and Breyer sought to clarify his position before Diamond spoke two additional (albeit meaningless) words—"Your Honor." Finally, a sympathetic Chief Justice John Roberts drew chuckles from the gallery when he told Diamond, "I think you're handling these questions very well." Ruth Bader Ginsburg immediately followed the laughter and made it clear the justices were not at all concerned with Diamond's view on this point: "That was not a question addressed to you, Mr. Diamond."[1]

Danforth raises a number of questions. Did the justices converse with and interrupt one another during this case in ways they usually do not? Or does *Danforth* give insight into how justices usually interact with each other when they discuss cases in open court? And if justices interrupt one another in systematic ways, why do they do so?[2] For example, is a conservative justice (Scalia) more likely to interrupt a liberal justice (Breyer) and vice versa (Stevens jumping in to respond to Scalia) because of their ideological distance from one another? In addition, do justices punish those who interrupt them or punish colleagues who regularly talk too much during these proceedings?

In this chapter, we seek to answer these questions by determining the extent to which justices behave in a manner similar to *Danforth* across cases and over time. First, we discuss why interruptions during conversations are theoretically important to decision making and how they affect interactions as people work to make decisions. We then show how this framework applies to the U.S. Supreme Court. From there, we employ an original data set to describe the nature of justices' interactions with one another during oral arguments. We provide descriptive data on justices' speaking patterns as well as on their interrupting behavior from the 1998 term to the 2007 term. From these data, as well as from our theoretical argument, we posit several testable hypotheses about the conditions under which we expect justices to speak over (interrupt) their colleagues during oral arguments. Finally, we present our results and make several observations about coalition formation and the phenomenon of interruptions during Supreme Court oral arguments.

Group Conversations, Interruptions, and Oral Arguments

Sociologists, economists, and psychologists have long studied the way in which humans interact with and react to one another in a group decision-making context. Indeed, chapter 1 illustrates that face-to-face communication may be the most important part of a decision-making process. At the same time, evidence suggests that initial communication sets the terms of debate for the discussion. But these are not the only aspects of communication and coalition formation that may affect how groups make decisions.

This chapter focuses on how actors treat each other during discussions and as they begin to form decisional coalitions. Specifically, we seek to determine why Supreme Court justices interrupt one another during oral argument discussions. To do so, we turn to sociological literature that analyzes group conversations and the reasons why those involved in such conversations may interrupt when someone else is speaking.

We first examine how conversations with others affect decision-making processes. Sociologists generally argue that when people speak within a group discussion context, they do so to "accomplish interactional goals or to block others from accomplishing theirs" (Kollock, Blumstein, and Schwartz 1985, 425). More specifically, communication is a tool used by people to accomplish goals and to coordinate their actions (Kanki, Folk, and Irwin 1991). Communication also enables people to state their intentions and to send and receive information from other group members (van der Kleij et al. 2009).

Put in political science terms, actors speak in an effort to move conversations toward their preferred outcome or at least to ensure that a decision will not be moved toward a less desirable outcome. Supreme Court justices sitting at oral arguments attempt to control the direction of discussion by asking questions or by making statements about how they view the case. In so doing, they begin the process of building coalitions with like-minded colleagues while keeping at bay those who are unlikely to join this coalition.

In response to people who want to move a discussion toward issues they prefer to discuss, another group member may interrupt. Smith-Lovin and Brody (1989) explain that such interruptions are meant to prevent a particular speaker from completing a thought or from accomplishing interactional goals (which in our terms means coalition-formation goals). In addition, interruptions may disorganize people's speech and ultimately their ideas (West 1979). The key to this literature is that by interrupting the current speaker, another member of a group discussion can change the entire dynamic of a decision-making process. In other words, while communication is generally meant to convey specific information in a group decision-making process, interruptions are meant to alter the topic or overall dynamic of the conversation. Doing so may, in turn, alter the group's ultimate decisions.

During Supreme Court oral arguments, interruptions may allow justices to thwart colleagues' lines of questioning in two ways. First, interruptions can keep speaking justices from signaling their intentions and preferred outcomes. That is, interrupting justices stop speakers in their tracks and allow interrupters to move the discussion to another topic. Second, interruptions keep speakers from sending signals to those with whom they hope to coordinate when the Court reaches a final decision. The bottom line is that interrupting justices while they are asking questions or making comments may be an effective strategy during oral arguments.

We note one caveat to this discussion. Sociologists suggest that interruptions "represent a clear violation of turn-taking norms" (Smith-Lovin and Brody 1989, 425). Given that Supreme Court justices clearly have a norm of collegiality with one another (Maltzman, Spriggs, and Wahlbeck 2000), we expect that interruptions will not remain unnoticed. That is, violating this norm may lead to retribution by other speakers.

The Nature of Interruptions during Oral Arguments

To gain empirical leverage on the general nature of how justices converse with one another during oral arguments as well as when and why they interrupt each other during these proceedings, we turn to 681 cases decided by the Supreme Court during its 1998–2007 terms. The data set includes all orally argued cases during this time, which encompasses the final years of the Rehnquist Court and the first two terms of the Roberts Court. These recent cases are unique because their oral argument transcripts are voice-identified, allowing us to generate valuable insights about the modern-day Court that few other studies have been able to provide.[3]

For each case, we downloaded the voice-identified transcripts from the Oyez Project and counted the number of times each justice spoke during oral arguments. While we frequently use the term *question,* our unit of analysis might more accurately be called *justice utterances.* That is, we simply count the number of times each justice's name appears, regardless of the content that follows. For example, during argument in *Hudson v. Michigan* (2007), Breyer offered this gem: "Sorry, I have laryngitis. Can you hear me all right?" Hence, we capture both questions and comments made from the bench. This process yielded a total of 87,941 justice utterances across our cases. Consistent with Johnson's (2004) findings, our results show that the justices collectively ask an average of 133 questions per case, or more than two per minute of oral argument.[4] The unmistakable conclusion is that the justices ask many questions and often make it difficult for the attorneys to work through their prepared arguments.[5] This finding is also consistent with the way both attorneys and justices view these proceedings (see chapter 1).

To better understand how often justices speak and interrupt each other, we used a computer script that assessed whether, for each utterance made by a justice, the speaker immediately preceding was also a member of the Court. This, then, is our operationalization of an interruption. Every utterance in the oral argument transcripts begins with a description of who is speaking (e.g., Scalia) followed by a colon. As such, the computer script allowed us to count every time one of the nine justices' names appeared in the speaker section of an utterance after another justice's name appeared in the previous speaker section. While there is some noise in the data (an interruption that is one word or an "um," for example), this noise is random and the resulting data generally paint a clear picture of how the justices treat each other during oral arguments.[6] We next use these data to provide a descriptive understanding of justices' speaking and interrupting behavior during oral arguments.

Speaking Patterns of Supreme Court Justices during Oral Arguments

Before we can fully assess interruptions at the individual level, we analyze how often each of the justices in our sample speaks during oral arguments as well as how much each has to say. The intuition is that if we do not gain insight into justices' speaking patterns, we will not be able to determine how often they interrupt—or are interrupted by—their colleagues. Figure 1, a violin plot, begins by describing the overall frequency of utterances made by a justice in a single case. Across the x-axis, we portray the ten justices in our data for whom some distribution of the number of utterances exists.[7] Within the panel and above each justice's name is a smoothed density estimate that describes how many times each justice has spoken across our data.

For the most part, the number of times each of the justices in our sample speaks comports with conventional wisdom about their varied levels of verbosity. Specifically, Scalia's average—roughly twenty-seven per case—is significantly larger than the average for all of his colleagues. While he is the most frequent questioner during oral argument, Scalia is also, as evidenced by the relative flatness of his density estimate, among the most unpredictable in terms of his expected level of activity.[8] By contrast, based on his initial tendencies in nearly 170 cases, Samuel Alito appears to be far more consistent in his questioning behavior, as demonstrated by the comparatively compact nature of his density estimate. Scalia, somewhat unsurprisingly, also receives the dubious honor of being the overall most prolific questioner. Indeed, in two recent cases, he spoke more than one hundred separate times.[9]

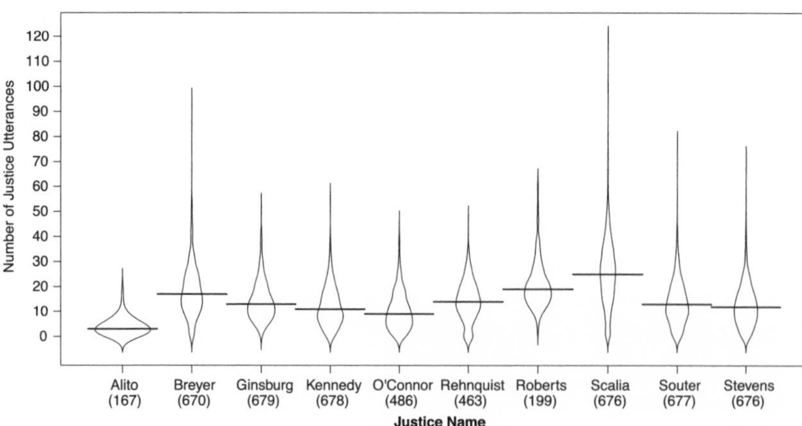

Fig. 1. Violin plot of justices' speaking frequencies. The solid horizontal bars within a specific density estimate provide the mean for a specific justice. The overall median across all justices is 14 utterances. Thomas, because of the infrequency with which he speaks, is not included in this figure (see note 13).

At the other end of the verbosity spectrum, Alito spoke less often than almost all other justices who sat during this time period. Indeed, in his first few terms on the bench, he spoke only 816 times in 167 cases (an average of 4.9 times per case). One possible explanation for this behavior is the freshman effect justices experience (Hagle 1993a). According to this theory, new justices act differently than their colleagues with more experience because they are simply getting used to the process on the nation's highest court. While the freshman effect may also apply to speaking during oral arguments, we cannot make a firm claim without testing it in a multivariate model.[10]

Alito's reticence to speaking is second only to Clarence Thomas's overall lack of activity at oral arguments. In fact, every question Thomas asks is an outlier. In other words, because he asks so few questions (an average approaching zero per case), any time he speaks is a notable exception (see, e.g., Sherman 2008). In one key instance, Thomas quite literally came to life during argument. In *Virginia v. Black* (2003), a case where the Court considered whether the First Amendment protects the right to burn a cross, he asked a number of pointed questions about how cross burning is not a form of speech but is meant only to terrorize its victims. He did so not by questioning the attorney who argued for the protection of cross burning but by prompting the attorney representing the U.S. government as amicus curiae to discuss the purpose of the anti-cross-burning law.

JUSTICE THOMAS: Mr. Dreeben, aren't you understating the—the effects of—of the burning cross? This statute was passed in what year?

MR. DREEBEN: 1952 originally.

JUSTICE THOMAS: Now, it's my understanding that we had almost one hundred years of lynching and activity in the South by the Knights of Camellia and . . . and the Ku Klux Klan, and this was a reign of terror and the cross was a symbol of that reign of terror. Was—isn't that significantly greater than intimidation or a threat?

MR. DREEBEN: Well, I think they're coextensive, Justice Thomas, because it is—

JUSTICE THOMAS: Well, my fear is, Mr. Dreeben, that you're actually understating the symbolism on—of and the effect of the cross, the burning cross. I—I indicated, I think, in the Ohio case that the cross was not a religious symbol and that it has—it was intended to have a virulent effect. And I—I think that what you're attempting to do is to fit this into our jurisprudence rather than stating more clearly what the cross was intended to accomplish and, indeed, that it is unlike any symbol in our society.

MR. DREEBEN: Well, I don't mean to understate it, and I entirely agree with Your Honor's description of how the cross has been used as an instrument of intimidation against minorities in this country. That has justified fourteen states in treating it as a distinctive—

JUSTICE THOMAS: Well, it's—it's actually more than minorities. There's certain groups. And I—I just—my fear is that the—there was no other purpose to the cross. There was no communication of a particular message. It was intended to cause fear and to terrorize a population.[11]

This exchange represented a veritable outburst for Thomas, and for good reason: This was an issue about which he cared greatly. Nevertheless, Thomas believes that justices should rarely speak during arguments and has publicly defended his failure to speak up more often: "[W]hy do you beat up on people if you already know [how you will decide based on the briefed arguments]? I don't know, because I don't beat up on 'em. I refuse to participate. I don't like it, so I don't do it" (Reeves 2009).

Understanding the dynamic of how often each justice speaks during

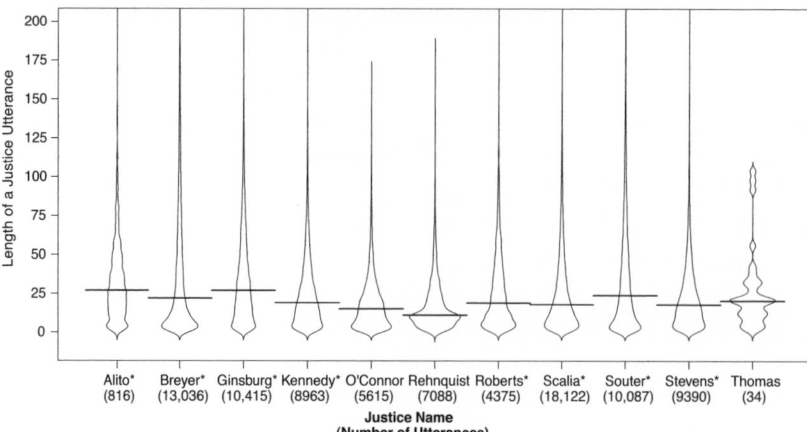

Fig. 2. Violin plot of justices' utterance length. The solid horizontal bars within a specific density estimate provide the mean for a specific justice. The overall median across all utterances and justices is 19 words. Justices with an asterisk after their name indicate that they have at least one utterance longer than 200 words, which we exclude to make the figure more visually useful.

oral arguments is only part of the story. We are also interested in the verbosity of the questions and comments they make. Figure 2 presents these data. As with the number of questions asked, variation occurs in the number of words used by the justices; some simply have more to say than others. While Scalia took top honors for both the largest number of questions asked and the highest overall average across all cases, the length of his utterances is right around the overall average of twenty or so words. Indeed, he is significantly less verbose than several of his colleagues, including Alito, Ginsburg, and David Souter.

As the figure also makes clear, some justices are more predictably verbose than others. For example, the figure shows a relatively thick density estimate for Alito, implying that a larger percentage of his utterances will be fifty or more words than will be the case for, say, Sandra Day O'Connor, whose upper-level values are relatively infrequent. Finally, the majority of justices in our data demonstrate the ability to go off the deep end in loquaciousness. For the sake of visual clarity, the figure has an upper bound of two hundred words for a single utterance, but eight of the eleven justices in our data had at least one utterance that exceeded that number. Breyer and Souter, who account for all of the ten longest utterances in our data, share top honors for the longest single utterances.[12]

Why is it important to understand how often justices speak and how long their utterances are when they choose to speak? Existing literature provides a partial answer. In his analysis of oral argument during the Burger Court era, Johnson (2004) reveals that the justices, rather than counsel, dominate these open court sessions. Such domination affects case outcomes, as the number of questions asked of each side significantly impacts who will win the case. In particular, the side that is asked more questions at oral arguments is unlikely to win the case (Johnson et al. 2009); as the differential between two sides increases, so, too, does the likelihood of winning/losing.

Interruptions at the Aggregate Level

Given the amount of information justices seek during oral arguments about policy, precedent, the separation of powers, and the law (Johnson 2004), they appear to have little time to accomplish much else. Nevertheless, our data indicate that interruptions still play a role in these proceedings. At the aggregate level, about 6 percent of justices' utterances (5,182 out of approximately 88,000) occur after another justice has spoken but before an attorney has a chance to speak. This amounts to almost eight interruptions (with a standard deviation of approximately six interruptions) in the average hour-long oral argument session. The fact that there are ten potential speakers at any one time (i.e., the nine justices plus the arguing attorney), combined with the justices' norm of collegiality (Epstein and Knight 1998; Maltzman, Spriggs, and Wahlbeck 2000) and the short time allotted for arguments, means that justices seem to use interruptions while making sure to avoid dominating the entire session.[13]

Although only a minority of justices' utterances meet our definition of an interruption, these interactions play a role in almost every case. Indeed, only 5 percent of the cases in our sample have no interruptions at all. In addition, in some cases, justices simply cannot stop themselves from speaking over one another. For example, with a total of fifty-seven interruptions during a single hour of oral argument, *Cheney v. U.S. District Court for the District of Columbia* (2004) has the most direct interactions between justices in our data.

Beyond this overall snapshot of how often justices interrupt one another, consider also term-by-term comparisons of this behavior. The first term in our analysis, 1998, has the highest percentage of justice utterances that we deem to be interruptions. Indeed, more than 9 percent of the time during this term, when a justice spoke, he or she was immediately preceded by a colleague. This figure is almost double the percentage for 2000 and 2001 and almost three times that for the 2006 and 2007 terms. Attorneys standing at the lectern during the 1998 term were clearly less a part of the "conversation" between bench and bar than what occurred during any other term in our analysis.

While variation exists over the remainder of the Rehnquist Court, the justices continued with a relatively high level of interruptions. This number ranged from an average of 4.74 per case in 2001 to 7.81 per case in 2003. This level dropped precipitously (and systematically when compared to the 1998 level) during the 2006 and 2007 terms. In particular, justices interrupted each other only an average of 3.52 times per case in 2006 and 3.68 times per case during 2007. This drop is consistent with both media and scholarly accounts of a markedly different collegial atmosphere during the first years of the Roberts Court (Totenberg 2006). While these aggregate results ultimately speak to this important question of collegiality, the real advantage our data provide is their ability to shed light on the behavior and relationships among the individual justices. We now turn to this analysis.

Interruptions at the Individual Level

The aggregate data paint a picture of how often justices interrupt one another on the late Rehnquist and early Roberts Courts. However, the data do not provide any information about how often particular justices are interrupted or how often each justice interrupts specific colleagues. Figure 3 provides an assessment of how justices treat one another when they make comments or ask questions.

The x-axis provides an indicator of a justice's politeness toward his or her colleagues during oral arguments. Specifically, it delineates the percentage of time each justice in our sample interrupts another justice. As with the number of questions asked, clear variation exists in the extent to which justices exhibit interrupting behavior. Alito, for example, is the least likely to butt in on someone else while he or she is speaking. Only 2.08 percent of the 816 questions he asked came immediately after another one of his colleagues had begun to speak. Alito consequently seems the most polite and the most deferential justice in our sample (although we have only slightly more than one term of data for him); none of his colleagues come close to his small percentage of interruptions. Indeed,

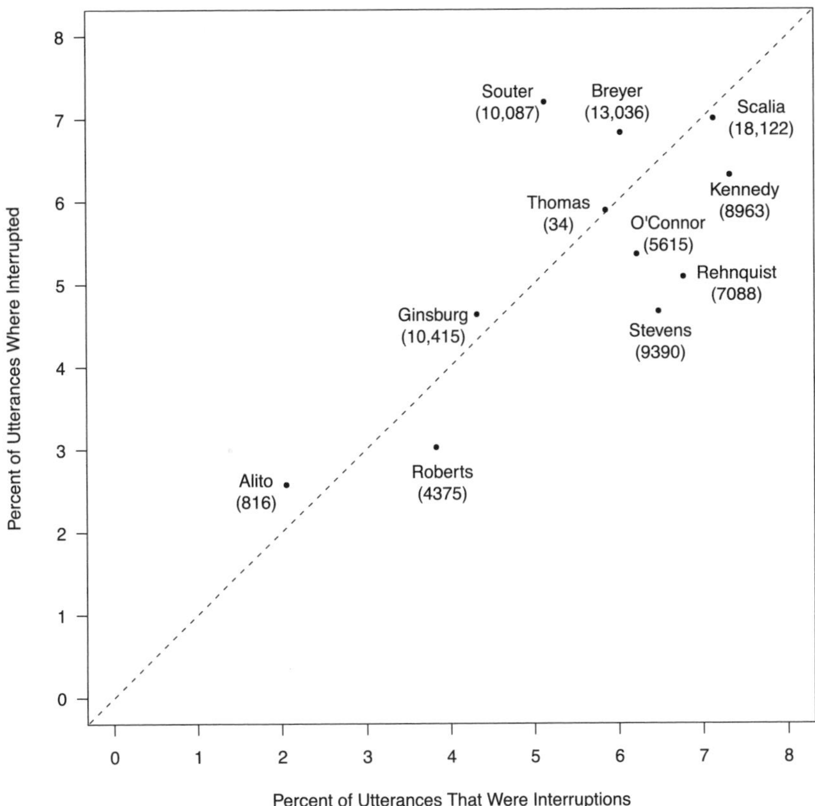

Fig. 3. Justices' pattern of interrupting others and of being interrupted. Dot plot of each justice's utterances during oral arguments (1998–2007). The *x*-axis is the percentage of a justice's utterances that interrupt another colleague. The *y*-axis is the percentage of utterances where a justice is the victim of an interruption.

his closest colleague, Roberts, interrupts his colleagues at almost double Alito's rate.

Just over a quarter of the justices in our sample find themselves in the middle of the continuum represented on the x-axis of figure 3, as Roberts, Ginsburg, and Souter fall into this category. Roberts hovers around 4 percent, Ginsburg uses only about 5 percent of her utterances to speak over her colleagues' questions and comments, and Souter interrupts others at the same rate as Ginsburg.

The majority of our justices end up on the right portion of the x-axis continuum (defined as more than 6 percent interruptions), which means

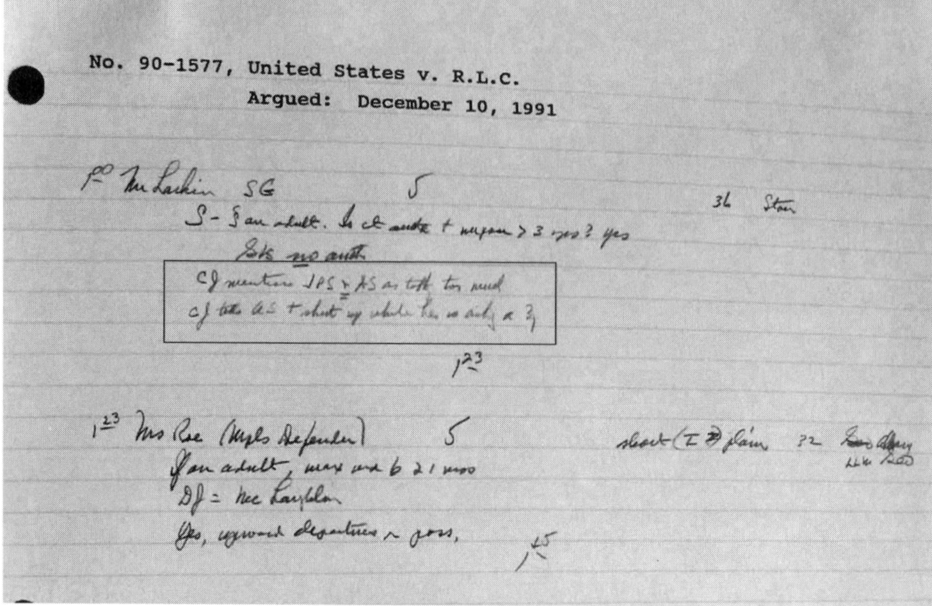

No. 90-1577, United States v. R.L.C.
Argued: December 10, 1991

Fig. 4. Justice Blackmun's notes in *U.S. v. R.L.C.* Blackmun's note concerning the Chief's response to Justice Scalia is on the fifth line of his notes about Mr. Larkin's argument. It is written in pencil and is marked with the box. (A color reproduction of these notes can be found via the link at http://www.press.umich.edu/titleDetailDesc.do?id=4599894.)

many of them seem particularly willing to speak over their colleagues. The two "rudest" of the justices are Anthony Kennedy and Scalia. Specifically, the data indicate that more than 7 percent of Kennedy and Scalia's utterances interrupt colleagues trying to ask questions or to make points to counsel. Such behavior does not always go unpunished. Indeed, in *U.S. v. R.L.C.* (1991), Rehnquist began to ask a question of counsel and Scalia spoke almost immediately. In his oral argument observations of the case, displayed in figure 4, Harry Blackmun noted the chief's irritation: "CJ tells AS t[o] shut up while he is asking a q[uestion]."

While the chief justice used tamer language than Blackmun indicated,[14] the point is the same—justices are sometimes annoyed by their colleagues' desire to speak over others on the bench. Ironically, Rehnquist was something of a serial interrupter. Indeed, close to 7 percent of his utterances began while another colleague was speaking. Even the justice viewed as the most polite, Stevens, had a penchant for interrupting colleagues: Almost

6.5 percent of his utterances fall into this category.[15] Finally, Breyer, O'Connor, and Thomas (barely) make it into this top category.[16]

Figure 3 certainly illustrates which justices are the most likely to speak over their colleagues. But, as the y-axis demonstrates, it also gives insight into which justices are the most likely to be the victims of interruptions. We make several observations based on these data. First, while a conservative majority reigned during the terms in our sample, justices from across the ideological spectrum were interrupted by their colleagues. Indeed, justices who were liberal (Breyer and Souter), moderate (Kennedy), and conservative (Scalia) were all interrupted at least 6 percent of the time when they spoke. The remainder of the justices in our sample had their questions or comments interrupted about 5 percent of time.

Second, the two newest justices in our sample, Roberts and Alito, were the least interrupted justices during their first full term together on the Court (2006). The newly appointed chief was interrupted only about 3 percent of the time. Alito experienced this phenomenon even less often—just over 2.5 percent of his questions or comments were interrupted. While we cannot give an exact explanation based on these bivariate data, it is possible that the other justices gave some deference to the two newcomers to the bench. This argument resembles our contention about the relationship between the freshman effect and justices' propensity to interrupt their colleagues.

A third notable trend in figure 3 is the apparent congruence between a justice's tendency to interrupt a colleague and the probability that other colleagues will interrupt that justice. For example, Alito interrupts his colleagues with just 2 percent of his utterances, and he, in turn, is only interrupted about 2.5 percent of the time when he speaks. In contrast, more than 7 percent of Scalia's utterances interrupt a colleague, and the other eight justices combined interrupt almost 7 percent of his speaking turns. This bivariate relationship is statistically significant and suggests that justices who dish it out to their colleagues must also be able to take it.[17]

Fourth, while figure 3 does not provide these data, we compare the relationship between our phenomenon of interest and the verbosity of the justices on the late Rehnquist and early Roberts Courts. Unsurprisingly, justices who are cut off by their colleagues have shorter questions and comments than when they are not interrupted. Across all justices, uninterrupted utterances average thirty words (standard deviation of 33.6), while interrupted utterances average only twenty-seven words (standard deviation 35.8). This difference is statistically significant ($p < 0.05$), which suggests that a selection effect is at work where the interrupted utterances

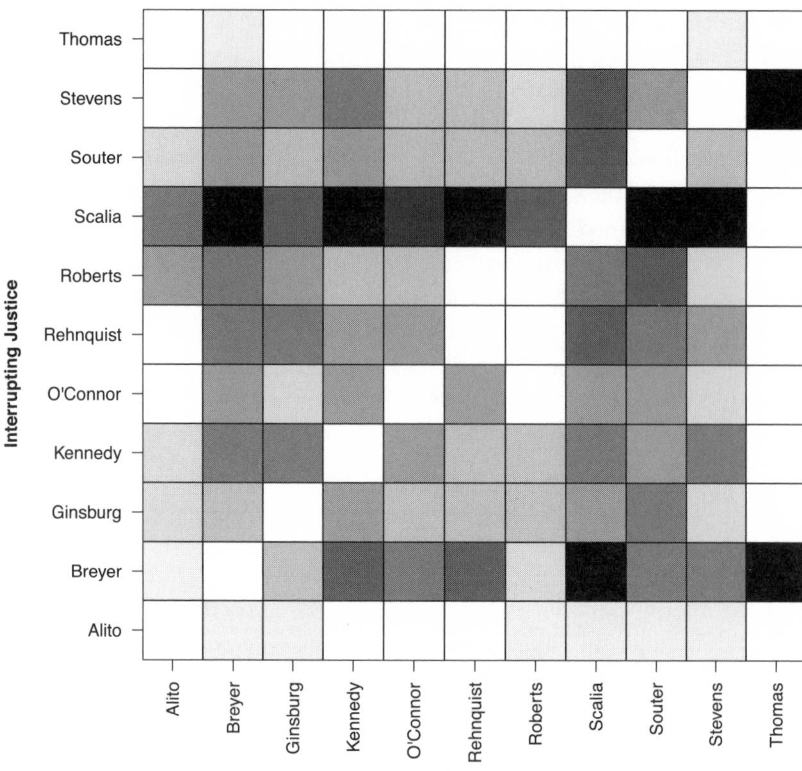

Fig. 5. Interruptions, interrupters, and justice pairings. Justice pairings show which justice interrupts which colleagues. The *y*-axis depicts the interrupting justice, and the *x*-axis depicts the justice being interrupted. The colors represent the level of interruptions. Black indicates a justice with high levels of interrupting a particular colleague while white indicates very few interruptions.

would be substantially longer if another justice had not begun speaking. In short, when justices are interrupted, their colleagues appear to exact punishment by cutting them off at the knees.

Figure 5 illustrates which justices are most apt to interrupt other specific colleagues. We examine each possible two-justice permutation on the Court. Each row presents one justice's interruptions of each of his or her colleagues. The shadings of the cells represent the percentage of a speaking justice's utterances that interrupt another justice. Black cells indicate a justice's highest level of interrupting a specific colleague, while white cells indicate the lowest level. The various shades of gray represent levels between the extremes.

As with figure 3, figure 5 paints an interesting picture of how certain justices interact with their colleagues. While variation exists, clear ideological patterns are present, as some justices are unabashed in who they interrupt while others reserve most of their interruptions for a few of their colleagues. Scalia interrupts everyone except Thomas (probably because he speaks so little and because they are such strong ideological allies) and reserves the bulk of his interruptions for ideological adversaries—Breyer, Souter, and Stevens. Moreover, Scalia interrupts the two key swing justices, O'Connor and Kennedy, at similar rates. This strategy seems odd, as either O'Connor or Kennedy was usually needed to secure a conservative majority. Breyer, too, reserves the majority of his interruptions for ideological antagonists. Indeed, he is most likely to interrupt Scalia, Thomas, Kennedy, O'Connor, and Rehnquist. Breyer interrupts Souter and Stevens to some extent but almost never interrupts Ginsburg. Anomalously, Scalia was also prone to interrupt Rehnquist, an ideological ally.

The other justices follow the Breyer/Scalia ideological pattern. Stevens and Souter interrupt Kennedy and Scalia, while Rehnquist focuses his interruptions on Breyer and Ginsburg. Roberts, for his part, is more likely to interrupt Souter and Breyer. Finally, Kennedy focuses on Breyer, Ginsburg, and Stevens. At the same time, he is also willing to interrupt O'Connor and Scalia. The former relationship may result from the fact that Kennedy and O'Connor shared the "swing justice" label and may have been fighting over the Court's policy choice in the final opinion. The latter relationship may result from the commonly held belief that O'Connor and Scalia simply did not get along with one another (see, e.g., Tarpley 2001; Toobin 2007).

This last point leads to the other relationship we can discern from figure 5: Justices are likely to interrupt colleagues who interrupt them. For example, Scalia's focus on Breyer seems to coincide with Breyer's focus on Scalia. In short, these two justices appeared to try to get even with one another. A similar pattern exists between Kennedy and Stevens, Stevens and Scalia, Roberts and Souter, Rehnquist and Scalia, and Scalia and O'Connor. These final two relationships involve ideological allies but seem to follow the pattern that justices are likely to punish colleagues who regularly interrupt them.

The ideological and "get even" relationships between justices are found in both high-profile and more mundane cases heard by the Court. Consider first what we deem "ideological interruptions" in one of the Court's most infamous cases of the past twenty-five years—*Bush v. Gore* (2000). This case, which essentially decided the 2000 presidential election, also demonstrates how the outcome of the case began with the oral arguments. Indeed, the justices sparred with one another throughout these proceedings, including maybe the quickest interruption of all time. Just over one minute into Theodore Olson's argument (on behalf of George W. Bush), Ginsburg began a question whose content we will never know. As she began to talk. Kennedy immediately asked his own question pertaining to jurisdiction:

MR. OLSON: Mr. Chief Justice, thank you, and may it please the Court. Just one week ago, this Court vacated the Florida Supreme Court's November 21 revision of Florida's election code, which had changed statutory deadlines, severely limited the discretion of the State's chief election officer, changed the meaning of words such as shall and may into shall not and may not, and authorized extensive standardless and unequal manual ballot recounts in selected Florida counties. Just four days later, without a single reference to this Court's December 4 ruling, the Florida Supreme Court issued a new, wholesale post-election revision of Florida's election law. That decision not only changed Florida election law yet again, it also explicitly referred to, relied upon, and expanded its November 21 judgment that this Court had made into a nullity.

JUSTICE GINSBURG: Mr. Olson—

JUSTICE KENNEDY: Can you begin by telling us our federal jurisdiction, where is the federal question here?

MR. OLSON: The federal question arises out of the fact that the Florida Supreme Court was violating Article II, section 1 of the Constitution, and it was conducting itself in violation of section 5 of Title III of federal law.[18]

Later in Olson's argument, Kennedy was at it again. This time he attempted to interrupt Souter as he was asking Olson about the Florida secretary of state's involvement in the case. Unlike his interruption of Ginsburg, however, this time Kennedy was apologetic and deferential.

JUSTICE KENNEDY: I understand that she has the expertise and let's assume that under Florida law she's the one with the presumptive competence to set the standard. Is there a place in the Florida scheme for [the secretary of state] to do this in the contest period?

MR. OLSON: I don't think there is.

JUSTICE KENNEDY: Even in the contest period?

MR. OLSON: I don't—I think that that's correct. Now, whether or not if there was a change as a result of that, of the process, whether there would be problems with respect to section 5 I haven't thought about, but—

JUSTICE KENNEDY: No, if there's—

JUSTICE SOUTER: If this were remanded—

JUSTICE KENNEDY: Go ahead. I'm sorry.

JUSTICE SOUTER: If this were remanded to the Leon County Circuit Court and the judge of that court addressed the Secretary of State, who arguably either is or could be made a party, and said please tell us what the standard ought to be, we will be advised by your opinion, that would be feasible, wouldn't it?[19]

It was not only the more conservative justices who chose to interrupt their colleagues at various points during the arguments in *Bush v. Gore.* When David Boise, arguing for Al Gore, was questioned by Kennedy and Scalia about the certification of the election results, Scalia interrupted Kennedy, Kennedy tried to interrupt Scalia, and in the cacophony Breyer jumped over both of the more conservative justices to make a key point:

MR. BOIES: But, but Your Honor, that is what happens every time there is a successful contest. The contest is a contest of the certification. You have the certification results first.

JUSTICE KENNEDY: It doesn't make any sense to me.

JUSTICE SCALIA: You have a certification which is made by the Secretary of State. That is what is contested.

MR. BOIES: Right.

JUSTICE SCALIA: And here the certification was directed to be changed.

JUSTICE KENNEDY: Let—

JUSTICE BREYER: By the way, does it matter if they said in Palm Beach and—Palm Beach and Miami-Dade, the ones that the court said you must certify, if they were thrown into the other—said recount them. If it's uncontested in the trial, I guess that you would get to the same place.

MR. BOIES: I think you get to exactly the same place.

JUSTICE BREYER: So it doesn't really matter.[20]

The ideological divide between the justices is only part of the explanation for the interruptions that took place in this case. Figures 3 and 5 indicate that justices seem to take revenge on one another if they are interrupted. In other words, there are instances where a justice interrupts a colleague, only to have the tables turned so that he or she is interrupted by the justice who was interrupted earlier. Indeed, Kennedy may have been trying to take such revenge in the preceding example.

A clearer instance of revenge-seeking behavior took place during another high-profile case, *McConnell v. FEC* (2003). *McConnell* dealt with the constitutionality of the Bipartisan Campaign Finance Reform Act, which, among other things, prohibited labor unions and corporations from using their general funds to engage in "electioneering communication." It also required comprehensive disclosure and record keeping related to such advertising. Beyond the important political implications of this decision (eventually overturned in *Citizens United v. FEC* [2010]), it nicely illustrates our point. Toward the end of Bobby Burchfield's argument (on behalf of the plaintiffs' political party), Scalia tried to make the point that the issue was one for the state party. Stevens interrupted him in a mistaken attempt to suggest that the issue was national in scope rather than involving the states:

JUSTICE SCALIA: Excuse me, is it an option for the national party or for the state?

MR. BURCHFIELD: It's not an option for the national party.

JUSTICE SCALIA: It's an option for the state party.

MR. BURCHFIELD: Exactly.

JUSTICE SCALIA: So a state party could destroy the—

JUSTICE STEVENS: It's an option for the national party because 323(b) is directed at the national parties.

MR. BURCHFIELD: 323(a) is directed to the national parties.

JUSTICE STEVENS: I'm sorry, you're right, it's a state thing.

MR. BURCHFIELD: And 323(a), as we've indicated, is an across-the-board criminal ban on national parties accepting any money that is not strictly regulated by FECA.[21]

While this interruption may have seemed innocuous, given that Stevens admitted that Scalia and Burchfield were right, Scalia still exacted some payback a few minutes later when Stevens attempted to ask a question of Olson but was ultimately forced to wait until Scalia finished his line of questioning.

JUSTICE STEVENS: General Olson—

JUSTICE SCALIA: Is that the problem you are solving here?

MR. OLSON: No, no, Justice Scalia. But it directly addresses the question that you raised to the extent that Congress was looking for a scheme to protect incumbencies, they were doing very well. It would be hard to develop a scheme that could be better for incumbents.

JUSTICE STEVENS: General Olson, I suppose another reason why we should not defer to the incumbents is they have an interest in spending their time working for the public rather than raising money, and this will save a lot of time so that we shouldn't defer to them on it, no.

MR. OLSON: The—that's, well—Justice Stevens. That's a reason for deferring to them.[22]

McConnell and *Bush v. Gore* illustrate that justices interrupt their ideological opponents and exact revenge on those adversaries who have interrupted them earlier in the proceedings. Furthermore, payback is not always reserved for adversaries. As we demonstrate in figure 4, Rehnquist not only showed his irritation with Scalia in *U.S. v. R.L.C.* but also was willing to interrupt him in other cases.

Consider *Hiibel v. Sixth Judicial District of Nevada* (2004), which focused on whether persons stopped by the police are required to give their name if asked for such information.[23] During oral arguments, the justices attempted to discern the extent to which the police may use investigative tools when they have stopped a suspect. Shortly into Robert Dolan's argument on behalf of Hiibel, Scalia responded to Dolan's contention that the police can run a car's license plate, but Rehnquist unabashedly jumped over Scalia to make a point:

MR. DOLAN: Yes, Your Honor. Certainly there are numerous investigative tools available to the police, including running the license plate. In fact, Deputy Dove—

JUSTICE SCALIA: Well, he does that. You—you—He does that and the person is—

CHIEF JUSTICE REHNQUIST: You can ask—you can ask if he's the owner of the car, the registered owner of the car, but you can't ask him his name?

MR. DOLAN: Well, we certainly believe that had that been the facts in the case and Mr. Hiibel chose not to respond, there would not be a basis that's proper under the law for a criminal prosecution in that regard, Your Honor.

The exchange did not end with the Scalia-Rehnquist incident. Rather, as the conversation continued, Souter spoke up but then seemed to realize he should not interrupt the chief. This time, however, Rehnquist (like Kennedy acted toward Souter in *Bush v. Gore*) was deferential.

JUSTICE SOUTER: Yes, but I thought—no. You were going to say something.

CHIEF JUSTICE REHNQUIST: That's all right. Go ahead.

JUSTICE SOUTER: I—I thought your position was that if it had been sufficiently apparent that Mr. Hiibel was associated with the truck, that he owned it, had been driving it or something like that, that under those circumstances, the—the police could have—could have exercised the State's regulatory power over motor vehicles and said, show me your driver's license or show me your registration. Is that correct?

MR. DOLAN: We believe that—that that is the law, Your Honor.[24]

Overall, these examples prompt several tentative observations. First, justices seem likely to interrupt those with whom they disagree ideologically. Second, they seek payback from those who interrupt other justices. Third, justices can and do interrupt their ideological allies if they show a penchant for interrupting others. Finally, justices may also at times show deference to one another.

Explaining Interruptions from the Bench

The theory behind conversations and interruptions, combined with our theoretical argument about coalition formation in chapter 1, leads us to several hypotheses regarding justices' interruption behavior during oral arguments. Because these literatures suggest that interruptions are meant to change the course of a discussion, these hypotheses focus on justices' ideological relationships with one another, the extent to which they punish colleagues who interrupt others, and case characteristics that may affect this phenomenon.[25]

First, it is now almost axiomatic that policy preferences play a key role in how Supreme Court justices make decisions. Some empirical evidence suggests that preferences alone explain how justices act (Rohde and Spaeth 1976; Segal and Spaeth 2002), while other scholars posit that justices simply try to maximize their policy goals (Epstein and Knight 1998; Maltzman, Spriggs, and Wahlbeck 2000). Either way, justices' ideological predispositions correspond with their actions and choices throughout the decision-making process. This belief also holds for oral arguments, where justices spar with one another and begin to zero in on the arguments used in their opinions. For example, Johnson, Wahlbeck, and Spriggs (2006) demonstrate that during oral arguments a justice is more likely to side with attorneys whose position is closer to his or her own ideal point. In addition, the evidence we provide in chapter 3 and the theory behind interruptions suggest that ideology may affect how justices interact with their colleagues during oral arguments. These factors lead us to the following hypothesis:

> *Hypothesis 1:* Justices are more likely to interrupt colleagues who are ideologically distant from them rather than those who are ideologically close to them.

Beyond the ideological relationship between justices, related reasons may explain why they interrupt one another during oral arguments. As they build coalitions, for example, justices use these proceedings to make points to their colleagues (see chapter 1). These points may be meant to be persuasive or to stake out policy territory as the court moves toward a final outcome.

Justices may instinctively seek to combat such persuasive efforts by interrupting a line of questioning to demonstrate problems with a point raised (as Stevens did in *McConnell*), to change the focus of discussion (as Kennedy did in *Bush v. Gore*), or simply to stop a colleague from proceeding with a particular line of questioning. The problem is that interrupting others breaks the norm of collegiality. In so doing, justices may raise their colleagues' ire.[26] For the phenomenon we examine here, the descriptive data in the previous section, combined with the sociological argument that interruptions violate norms of conversations, indicates that such is the case, as justices who interrupt others seem to be interrupted more often themselves. Furthermore, specific justices seem to exact revenge against those who are more willing to interrupt them. This behavior, along with the concept that justices punish those who break the norm of collegiality, leads us to two predictions:

> *Hypothesis 2a:* A justice who interrupts a specific colleague is more likely to be interrupted by that colleague later in the oral arguments.

Hypothesis 2b: Justices who interrupt anyone during oral arguments are more likely to be interrupted by any of their colleagues later in the proceedings.

Justice- and case-level characteristics may also affect justices' propensity to interrupt colleagues. We turn first to justices, focusing on the extent to which they are experts on the issue being argued in a given case. Existing work provides evidence that issue experts are more likely to receive opinion assignments than colleagues with less experience (Maltzman and Wahlbeck 2004). This finding suggests that justices defer to these issue experts because they simply know more about a given case area than do their colleagues. This leads us to hypothesize:

Hypothesis 3a: Justices are less likely to interrupt a colleague who is an issue expert in a case.

At the same time, when speaking justices are not experts in a particular issue, their colleagues may feel like they have the right to interrupt because they know more about the issues involved than anyone else on the bench. In particular, issue experts may believe it is their duty to make sure everyone properly understands the case. As a result, these issue experts may be more likely to interrupt colleagues viewed as moving the discussion away from where it should be going. As such, we also hypothesize:

Hypothesis 3b: Justices who are issue experts are more likely to interrupt other colleagues who have less experience in the issue area of the case.

Case complexity plays a role at many points of the justices' decision-making process (see, e.g., Maltzman, Spriggs, and Wahlbeck 2000). It may also affect justices' inclination to interrupt their colleagues. Indeed, because there are so many more issues in a complex case (Collins 2008b), the justices' cognitive attention should be focused on understanding their positions and on formulating questions rather than on engaging in verbal combat with their colleagues. While complex cases may seem ripe for framing or agenda setting, because of the time constraints at oral argument justices' first priority is to understand the basic issues of a case. In other words, justices must figure out their positions before attempting to shape their colleagues' preferences. As such, we posit:

Hypothesis 4: Justices are less likely to interrupt any of their colleagues as the complexity of a case increases.

Finally, we know that when justices speak more during oral arguments, they often tip their hands about how they will vote in the case (Johnson et al. 2009). But how might the verbosity we describe in the previous section relate to justices' willingness to interrupt their colleagues? We suggest that such behavior is linked to the concept of punishment. However, instead of punishing a colleague for being rude as a consequence of past interruptions, the punishment is leveled at someone who is particularly verbose. This is akin to Rehnquist telling Scalia to calm down and let other justices have a chance to speak. Based on this argument, we hypothesize:

Hypothesis 5: Justices are more likely to be interrupted as the verbosity of their questions/comments increases.

Data and Methods

To test these hypotheses, we return to the 681 cases described earlier. The unit of analysis, however, is not each case. Rather, because interruptions take place between pairs of justices and may happen any time one of them speaks, our model focuses on each justice's response to every utterance made by another justice.[27] To illustrate this point, assume Scalia asks the first question or makes the first statement from the bench during oral argument in a given case. This utterance yields eight observations because we code for whether each colleague interrupted him. Hence, if he speaks one hundred times in a case, we include eight hundred Scalia-based observations for that case.[28] We then repeat this coding across all justice utterances and across all cases in our sample. Doing so yields a total of 694,496 observations. Because each observation is coded 1 if a justice interrupted an utterance and 0 otherwise, we employ a logistic regression model.[29]

The model includes several independent variables to test our hypotheses. First, to test how the ideological relationship between justices affects their propensity to interrupt someone else, we employ Martin and Quinn (2002) scores. Specifically, using their dynamic ideal point scores, we take the absolute value of the difference between justices. This variable, *Ideological Distance*, ranges from .001 to 6.87, with a mean of 2.63 and a standard deviation of 1.70. As Hypothesis 1 posits, we expect larger values (meaning that the justice pairing is farther apart) to be correlated with a higher propensity of interrupting behavior.

Second, we include two variables to determine how justices' actions during oral arguments affect the probability that they will be interrupted. To test our hypothesis that justices face payback when they interrupt a specific colleague, we include a variable, *Speaker Previously Interrupted Specific Colleague,* which is coded 1 if a justice previously interrupted the current speaker and 0 otherwise. We expect this variable to be positively correlated with our dependent variable. Similarly, we include a variable to determine whether justices enforce a norm of collegiality whereby they interrupt a justice who interrupted anyone else during a particular argument session. This variable, *Speaker Previously Interrupted Any Colleague,* is coded similarly to the previous variable.

Hypotheses 3a and 3b indicate that we are also interested in how justices' expertise in the issue area of a case affects whether their colleagues interrupt them and whether experts are more likely to interrupt others. For each variable, *Colleague's Issue Expertise* and *Speaker's Issue Expertise,* we tabulated the (rolling) percentage of opinions in an issue area in which each justice authored an opinion prior to the current case. Hence, higher values are associated with more expertise, whereas lower values indicate less experience in a particular issue area.

We code *Case Complexity* according to Collins (2008b) as the total number of amicus curiae briefs submitted in a case. The logic is that as more briefs are submitted, the justices must grapple with more potential issues. We expect fewer interruptions in more complex cases because the justices may be more focused on the issues rather than on what their colleagues are doing during oral arguments. This variable ranges from 0 to 89 and has a mean of just over 7 briefs per case, with a standard deviation of 9 briefs.

Finally, we determine whether a justice's verbosity affects the likelihood that her colleagues will interrupt her questions or comments. We code this variable, *Colleague's Previous Words,* as the total words used by the current speaker during the oral arguments prior to the specific observed utterance. It has a mean of 24.66 with a standard deviation of 8.49. Our expectation is that verbose justices are more likely to be interrupted by their colleagues. We also control for the number of words used by the current speaker so that we have an idea of how his or her verbosity affects the propensity that he or she will interrupt a colleague. This variable, *Speaker's Previous Words,* has a mean of 23.69, with a standard deviation of 8.68.

Results

Table 1 reports parameter estimates for our logistic regression model. Many variables are signed in the expected direction and are statistically significant. To understand the substantive significance of the results, however, we focus on predicted probabilities.

We begin with the first hypothesis—that justices are more likely to be interrupted by ideologically distant colleagues. Figure 6 indicates a clear positive effect between ideological distance and the propensity that a justice will interrupt a speaking colleague. Specifically, when a justice is the most ideologically similar to the speaker (e.g., Scalia and Thomas), the probability of an interruption occurring is about 0.005. This probability increases to almost 0.007 when the colleagues are the most distant from one another (e.g., Stevens and Scalia). While the probabilities are quite small, this finding results from the fact that there are only about five thousand total interruptions in our sample. That said, the relative change in probability demonstrated in this figure—a 40 percent increase—indicates that the ideological relationship between two justices is an important predictor of interruptions on the bench.

This relationship should come as no surprise. Ideological adversaries spar during conference (Frederick 2003), during the opinion-writing and bargaining process (Maltzman, Spriggs, and Wahlbeck 2000), and in the Court's final opinions. Thus, if, as we contend, these processes begin dur-

TABLE 1. When Is a Justice Interrupted by a Colleague?

	Coefficient	Robust S.E.
Ideological Distance	0.055*	0.009
Speaker Previously Interrupted Specific Colleague	3.046*	0.073
Speaker Previously Interrupted Any Colleague	0.449*	0.058
Colleague's Issue Expertise	0.013*	0.002
Speaker's Issue Expertise	–0.002	0.002
Case Complexity	–0.011*	0.002
Speaker's Previous Words	–0.000*	0.000
Colleague's Previous Words	0.001*	0.000
Constant	–5.652*	0.074
Observations	694,496	
Pseudo R^2	0.087	
Log likelihood	–27,874.158	

Note: Logistic regression model parameter estimates of whether a speaking justice is interrupted by one of her colleagues.

*denotes $p < 0.05$ (two-tailed test). Robust standard errors are clustered on each justice/case combination ($N = 6,056$).

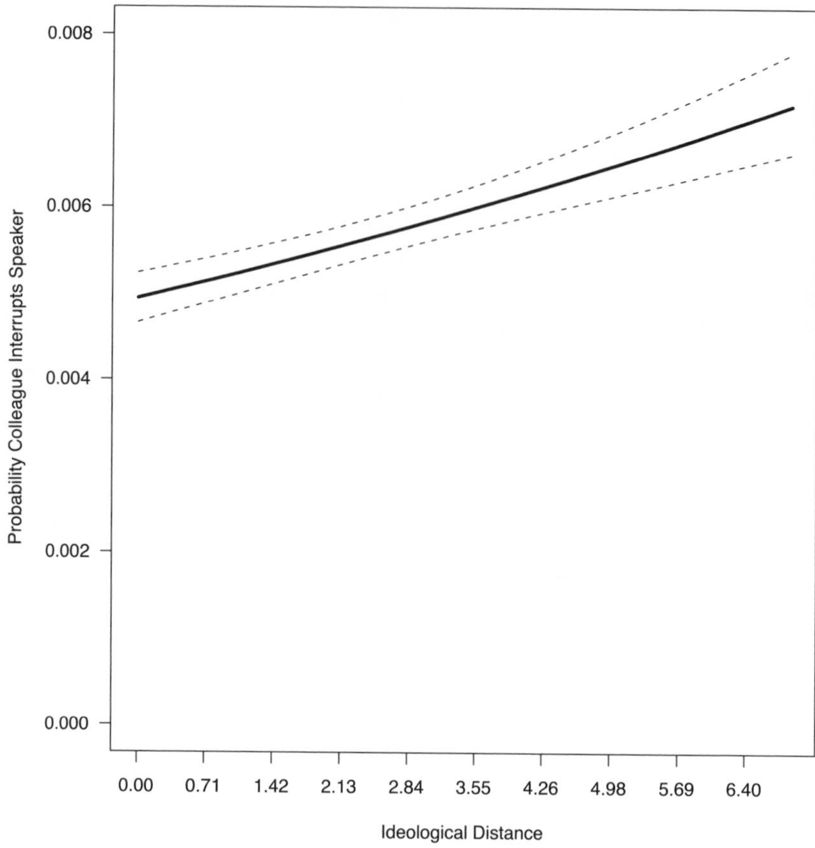

Fig. 6. Probability of interrupting a speaker based on ideology. Graph depicts the predicted probability that a specific colleague interrupts a speaking justice, conditional on the ideological distance between the two justices. All other variables were set at their mean or modal values, as appropriate. Point estimates (thicker line) and 95 percent confidence intervals (dashed lines) were generated through stochastic simulations similar to Clarify.

ing the oral arguments, it is natural that ideology would play a role here, too. The examples we provide earlier in this chapter certainly support this claim. Theoretically, if justices seek to make points prominently and to discount points with which they disagree, then interrupting adversaries may be a good way to do so.[30]

Ideological foes clearly interrupt one another at a rate higher than do allies. But beyond ideology, do justices enforce the Court's more general

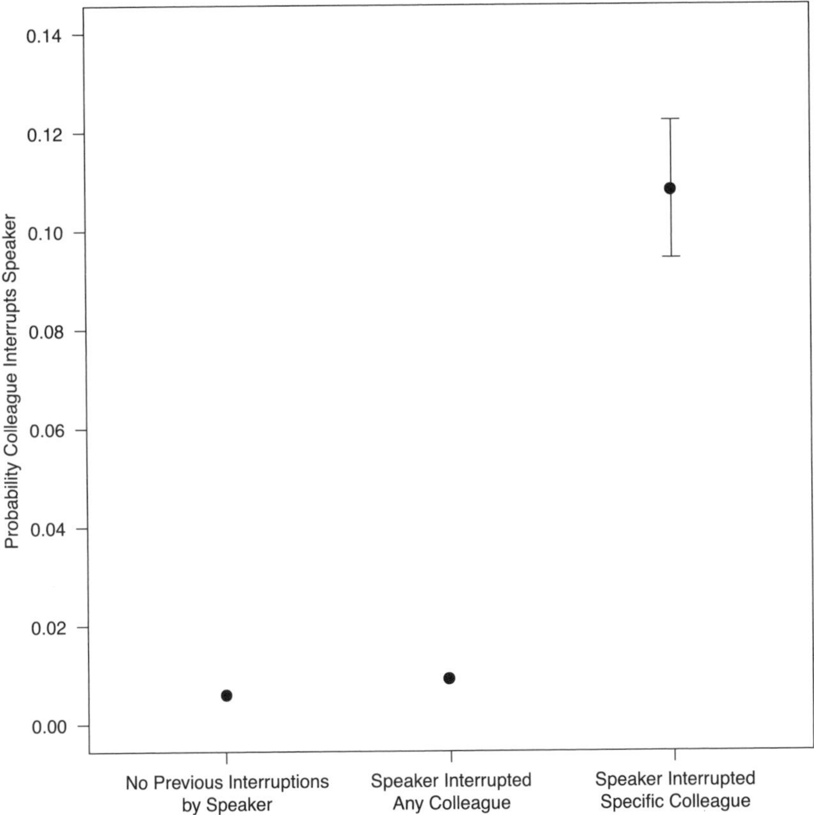

Fig. 7. Are interruptions conditional on past behavior? Graph depicts predicted probability that a specific colleague interrupts a speaking justice, conditional on the previous interruption behavior of the speaking justice. All other variables were set at their mean or modal values, as appropriate. Point estimates (dots) and 95 percent confidence intervals (whisker lines) were generated through stochastic simulations similar to Clarify. Note that the confidence interval for the "No Previous Interruptions" point is [0.005, 0.006] and the confidence interval for "Speaker Interrupted Any Colleague" point is [0.008, 0.01]. These whiskers do not show up on the figure because they are actually smaller than these two dots.

norm of collegiality during oral arguments? The parameter estimates in table 1 suggest that the answer is yes. Indeed, justices seem to be punished later in the proceedings by a justice whom they interrupted earlier. The rest of the Court also punishes interrupters. Despite these statistical relationships, as figure 7 makes clear, only a specific interruption has a substantively significant probability of leading to an interruption later in the argument session.

When justices speak but have not interrupted others prior to this utterance, there is only about a 1 percent probability that they will be interrupted. Comparing such instances to when justices interrupt colleagues is instructive. There is almost no increase in the probability that a particular justice will interrupt another justice if he or she interrupted any of the other justices during the proceedings. However, if a justice interrupted a specific colleague early in the session, the previously interrupted justice has about an 11 percent probability of gaining revenge. Revenge thus seems to be a personal issue for the justices rather than a norm-enforcing phenomenon.

While justices' relationships with one another affect whether they interrupt each other as they figure out how they will decide a case, individual and case-level characteristics also affect this phenomenon. We turn first to issue expertise. The left panel of figure 8 shows that the substantive effect of this variable is strong and clear. When justices have written almost no opinions in a particular issue area, there is less than a .5 percent probability that they will interrupt other justices in a case, but when justices have written extensively in an issue area, the probability more than triples. This finding is intuitive; justices seem to listen to experts at various points during their decision-making process, and they seem to do so during oral arguments as well. The bottom line is that experts garner some measure of respect from their colleagues.

At the same time, complex cases lead justices to interrupt each other less often than in more straightforward cases. The right panel of figure 8 demonstrates that as the number of amicus briefs increases from approximately one to fifty, the probability of an interruption drops by almost half. That is, when the justices have more issues with which to grapple, they may lack the time to spar with colleagues. Rather, we suspect that the justices may be more focused on making sure they have a clear grasp of all the issues and how they may lead to particular outcomes.

Finally, we find no support for our final hypothesis. Figure 9 indicates that contrary to our argument, a speaker's verbosity does not seem to affect whether she is interrupted by colleagues during oral arguments. That is, speakers are no more likely to be interrupted whether they use few or many words.

Conversely, figure 9 provides an interesting portrait of how word usage affects interruptions. When justices are verbose during argument sessions, they are more likely to interrupt other speakers. Specifically, as justices move from saying almost nothing to using almost thirty-five hundred

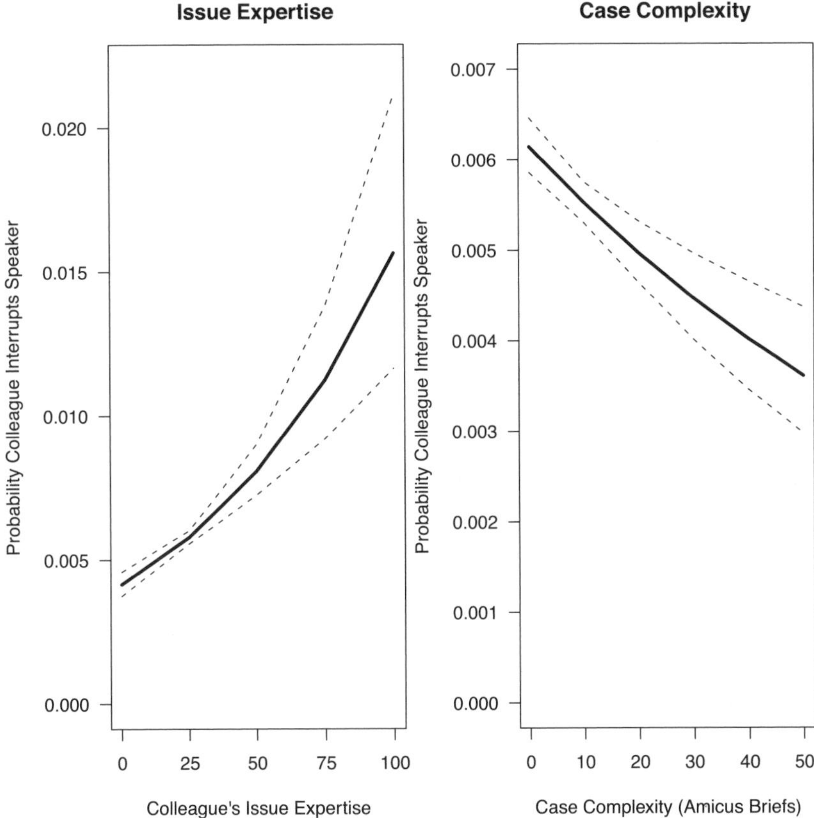

Fig. 8. Issue expertise, case complexity, and interruptions. Graphs represent predicted probability that a specific colleague interrupts a speaking justice, conditional on the level of issue expertise possessed by the specific colleague (*left panel*) and the level of case complexity (*right panel*). All other variables were set at their mean or modal values, as appropriate. Point estimates (thicker line) and 95 percent confidence intervals (dashed lines) were generated through stochastic simulations similar to Clarify.

words in a session, the probability that they will interrupt a colleague increases tenfold. This finding suggests that justices who dominate the proceedings also seem to run roughshod over their colleagues.

Conclusion

Former Supreme Court justice, solicitor general, and experienced advocate Robert H. Jackson once said that he gave three arguments in each

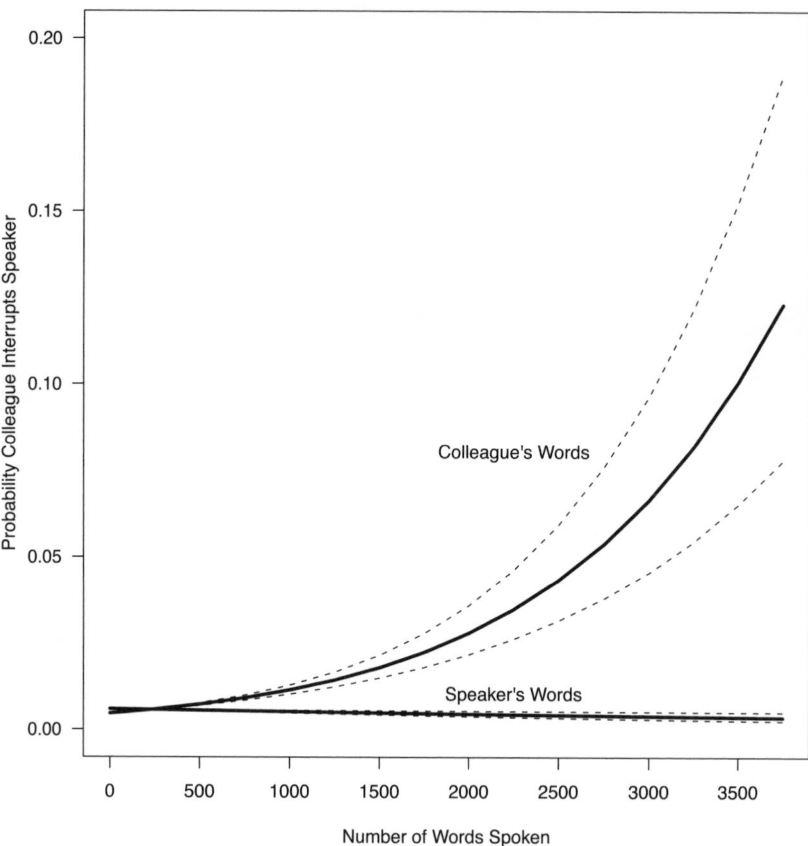

Fig. 9. Asymmetrical effect of verbosity on interruptions. Graph represents the predicted probability that a specific colleague interrupts a speaking justice, conditional on the number of words previously spoken by each justice. All other variables were set at their mean or modal values, as appropriate. Point estimates (thicker line) and 95 percent confidence intervals (dashed lines) were generated through stochastic simulations similar to Clarify.

case: "First came the one that I planned—as I thought, logical, coherent, complete. Second was the one actually presented—interrupted, incoherent, disjointed, disappointing. The third was the utterly devastating argument that I thought of after going to bed that night" (see Frederick 2003, 13). This chapter systematically documents the extent to which oral arguments resemble the second type of argument that Jackson outlined—interrupted and disjointed. To do so, we examined how justices behave during oral arguments and how they treat their colleagues during these proceedings.

What we find suggests that interruptions, which occur on average eight times per case, play a key role for the Court. In addition, these interruptions certainly have distinct patterns. Justices who take opposite ideological positions more frequently interrupt each other. At the same time, as at other stages of the decision-making process, justices enforce the norm of collegiality by punishing those who use interruptions as a strategy during oral arguments.

More generally, to understand the role and importance of interruptions, we have to take a step back and reiterate the purpose of oral arguments. These proceedings serve as an information-gathering device for the justices, where they acquire information about other justices' preferences and information that the parties or amici did not provide in the briefs (Johnson 2004). This information is vital because it enables justices to establish legal policy as close to their own personal policy preferences as possible (Johnson 2004).

Consistent with the information function of oral arguments, when justices ask attorneys questions, they do so in large part to signal their colleagues about issues viewed as important for deciding the case at hand. In chapters 1 and 3, we theorize about how justices use these proceedings to listen to each other, to gather information, and to employ such information to build coalitions. Accordingly, we posit that the key function of interruptions is to enhance or hinder other justices' learning processes with an eye toward the coalition-formation process. In other words, if a justice believes that a line of questioning may lead the Court toward an outcome out of line with his or her preferences, he or she may interrupt colleagues in an effort to disturb this process and ultimately affect the outcome of the case.

3 | Listen to Me: How Justices Learn during Oral Arguments

Chapter 1 laid out our general position that Supreme Court justices begin their coalition-formation process during oral arguments. Chapter 2 provided evidence from the past decade that the sparring in which justices engage follows systematic patterns. Specifically, justices are prone to interrupt the questions and comments of their colleagues with whom they probably most disagree. But those findings do not provide an answer to another, equally important, question: To what extent do justices take the time beyond trying to circumvent a line of questioning to listen to what their colleagues have to say? To answer this question, we move back in time to the Burger Court era and to two justices who left evidence of their listening ability—Lewis F. Powell and Harry A. Blackmun. Both men kept records of what transpired during oral arguments, including a treasure trove of notes about their colleagues.[1] Later in the chapter we describe in more detail these notes and the data we draw from them. For now, we provide but a taste of how Powell and Blackmun used them in one of the Court's most famous criminal cases, *Batson v. Kentucky* (1986).

The U.S. Supreme Court often confronts the most controversial issues in American society. On December 12, 1985, it heard oral arguments in *Batson*, a case that would ultimately place race and discrimination squarely in the Court's path. The legal question in *Batson* involved the use of peremptory challenges during voir dire (jury selection). On closer inspection, however, the case clearly and directly involved race, a critical issue in American politics. Specifically, it went straight to the core of every American's right to equal protection of the laws during jury trials.

The facts in *Batson* were straightforward. James Batson, a black man, was indicted and on trial for second-degree burglary and receipt of stolen goods. During the first day of trial, the judge conducted jury selection by questioning prospective jurors. At the time, the law allowed the parties to eliminate jurors for two reasons—for cause (based on an overt or known bias that was discovered during questioning) or on peremptory challenge (each side's power to excuse a certain number of jurors without giving a reason). After the judge excused various jurors for cause, the parties exercised their peremptory challenges to eliminate other jurors. The controversy arose when the prosecutor used his peremptory challenges to strike all four black individuals from the panel, leaving an all-white jury.

The defense attorney objected and wanted to discharge the jury before it was sworn on the grounds that the removal of the prospective black jurors violated Batson's rights under the Sixth and Fourteenth Amendments to a jury drawn from a cross-section of the community and under the Fourteenth Amendment guarantee of equal protection of law. The judge denied the petitioner's motion based on the reasoning that the cross-section requirement applies only to selection of the venire (the jury pool or panel from which juries are selected) and not to selection of the petit jury itself. Batson was later convicted on both counts, and the Kentucky Supreme Court affirmed the verdict on appeal.

As with the examples in the previous two chapters, we posit that the outcome of *Batson* began to form as the justices discussed the issues with one another during oral arguments. Unlike the analysis of justices' direct interactions in chapter 2, however, the exchanges we highlight here demonstrate how the conversational interactions during these proceedings provide justices with a valuable forum for making points to their colleagues; for learning about the questions, concerns, and preferences of their fellow justices; and for gauging their colleagues' views of how a case should be decided. During the opening few minutes of the petitioner's oral argument in *Batson,* it quickly became clear that the key controlling precedent was *Swain v. Alabama* (1965), with both the trial court and the Kentucky Supreme Court relying heavily on that case's tenets. *Swain* held that defendants are not constitutionally entitled to a proportionate number of members of their race on the trial jury or jury panel and that the prosecutor's striking of an entire race of individuals (African Americans in *Swain*) through the peremptory challenge system did not constitute denial of equal protection of the laws.

Thus, when the petitioners presented their written brief to the Supreme Court, they based the argument primarily on a Sixth Amendment claim and did not include a position on the Fourteenth Amendment. This approach did not resonate with Sandra Day O'Connor's view of the proper vehicle for resolving the case. She pressed J. David Niehaus, the attorney for the petitioner, on this point:

MR. NIEHAUS: The conventional interpretation of *Swain* is that there can be no question of peremptory challenges and the way that they are exercised in any one particular case. This has been the basis for decisions of the many state courts who have refused to consider the newer rules that have been advanced by the Supreme Court of California, the court in Massachusetts, and more recently by two federal appellate courts.

JUSTICE O'CONNOR: Mr. Niehaus, *Swain* was an equal protection challenge, was it not?

MR. NIEHAUS: Yes.

JUSTICE O'CONNOR: Your claim here is based solely on the Sixth Amendment?

MR. NIEHAUS: Yes.

JUSTICE O'CONNOR: Is that correct?

MR. NIEHAUS: That is what we are arguing, yes.

JUSTICE O'CONNOR: You are not asking for a reconsideration of *Swain,* and you are making no equal protection claim here. Is that correct?

MR. NIEHAUS: We have not made an equal protection claim. I think that *Swain* will have to be reconsidered to a certain extent if only to consider the arguments that are made on behalf of affirmance by the respondent and the solicitor general.[2]

At first glance, this exchange appears benign because it merely clarifies a section of the petitioner's brief containing an "equal protection analysis" that focused on how *Swain* "effectively ended the employment of the Equal Protection Clause to combat improper use of peremptory challenges by the prosecutor" (petitioner's brief, 21). But this exchange becomes more important when one thinks of oral arguments as a conversation between the justices and in light of how the Court ultimately decided *Batson.* In the majority opinion, the Court found that "the State's privilege to strike individual jurors through peremptory challenges, is subject to the commands of the Equal Protection Clause [and it] forbids the prosecutor to challenge potential jurors solely on account of their race" (majority opinion, 89). In essence, the point for us (following Johnson 2004) is that the majority opinion relied primarily on an argument that emerged from a question O'Connor raised during the petitioner's argument.

How do we know this? First, in his dissent, Chief Justice Warren E. Burger makes this point as he quotes the exchange between Niehaus and O'Connor (Burger's dissent, 112). Further, Powell, the eventual majority opinion writer, recorded this point in the notes he took during the arguments. Indeed, the next time O'Connor pushed this position, she clearly wanted to view the case through the lens of the Fourteenth Amendment:

JUSTICE REHNQUIST: Well, but I think at least speaking for myself I would like to know what the consequences, the logical consequences of adopting your rule are, and I take it if most state courts have adopted it and felt obliged to extend it to defendants, that might well be a logical consequence.

MR. NIEHAUS: Oh, I think that it could be, Your Honor, but the Court could also consider—

JUSTICE O'CONNOR: Well, how can you do that under a Sixth Amendment claim? I can understand how you could reach that result under an equal protection claim, which you aren't making, but I don't see how the Sixth Amendment does anything but speak to the defendant's own rights.

MR. NIEHAUS: This is quite right, Your Honor, but the courts that have addressed the matter and more recently the case in *Booker v. Jade* from the Sixth Circuit, which we have not had time to file with the Court, simply talks about fairness between the parties, and that it does tend to diminish the perception of fairness in the eyes of the public, and those courts have perceived a—I guess you would say a right emanating, although not specifically stated, out of the Sixth Amendment, wherein the courts may impose the same rule on the defendant in order to bring out the confidence necessary for—

JUSTICE O'CONNOR: Well, it certainly is doctrinally difficult to justify under the Sixth Amendment, isn't it?

MR. NIEHAUS: Yes, Your Honor.[3]

Figure 10, Powell's notes in *Batson,* takes us to the heart of the matter. On the second page, Powell wrote, "SO'C commented she could see no basis for a 6th amend. claim. Best basis would be E/P clause." In short, O'Connor was letting her colleagues know that she would not be a part of any coalition that relied solely on a Sixth Amendment claim. More generally, such exchanges during oral argument are conversations that illustrate the important issues in a case. Justices listen to one another during these proceedings to discern the issues that are important to their colleagues and that can later be used in the coalition-formation process. Powell was certainly listening to O'Connor, an important swing vote on the Court.

However, O'Connor was not the only justice to whom Powell paid attention in the courtroom that day. Indeed, another key player in the coali-

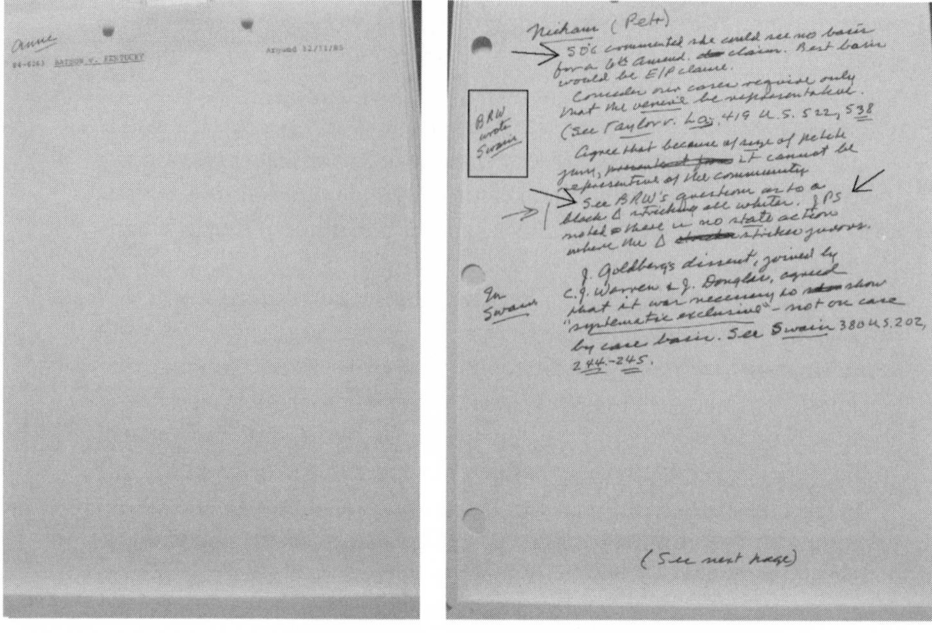

BATSON v. KENTUCKY

Nickens (Petr)

SOC commented she could see no basis for a 6th Amend. claim. Best basis would be E/P clause.

Concedes our cases require only that the venire be representative. (See Taylor v. La., 419 U.S. 522, 538

Agree that because of size of petit jury, it cannot be representative of the community.

See BRW's question as to a black Δ striking all whites. JPS noted there is no state action where the Δ strikes jurors.

J. Goldberg's dissent, joined by C.J. Warren & J. Douglas, agreed that it was necessary to show "systematic exclusion" – not on case by case basis. See Swain 380 U.S. 202, 244–245.

BRW wrote Swain

In Swain

(See next page)

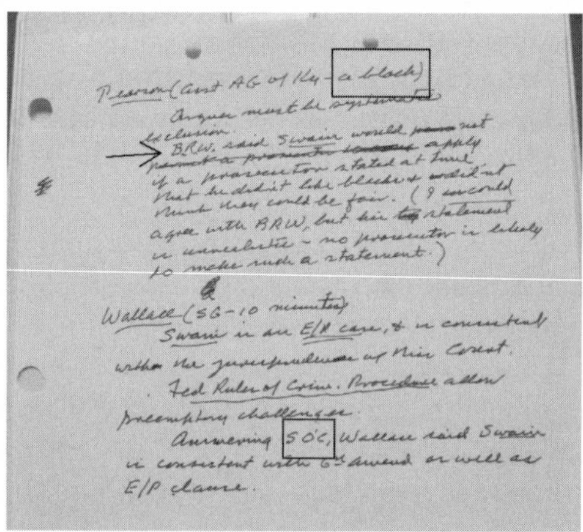

Pearson (Asst AG of Ky – a black)

Argues must be systematic exclusion.

BRW said Swain would not apply if a prosecutor stated at trial that he didn't like blacks & couldn't think they could be fair. (I would agree with BRW, but his statement is unrealistic – no prosecutor is likely to make such a statement.)

Wallace (SG – 10 minutes)

Swain is an E/P case, & is consistent with the jurisprudence of this Court.

Fed Rules of Crim. Procedure allow peremptory challenges.

Answering SOC, Wallace said Swain is consistent with 6th Amend as well as E/P clause.

Fig. 10. Justice Powell's notes from *Batson v. Kentucky.*
(A color reproduction of these notes can be found via the link at http://www.press.umich.edu/titleDetailDesc.do?id=4599894.)

tion-building game was Justice Byron R. White, who wrote the majority opinion in *Swain*. This fact was not lost on Powell, who wrote in the margin of the second page in figure 10, "BRW wrote *Swain*." Again, this notation may seem innocuous, but the point is that if Powell were to write the majority opinion in *Batson* and wanted to include White in his coalition, Powell would need to know what issues were important to White. Unsurprisingly, Powell went beyond reminding himself that White wrote *Swain*. Rather, he paid particular attention to White's (and in fact John Paul Stevens's) concerns about the equal protection analysis.[4] Consider the exchange that took place among White, Stevens, and Niehaus as well as how O'Connor raised the possibility that the Court might still be able to use an equal protection challenge to alleviate any problems with this position.

JUSTICE WHITE: How about the black defendant striking white jurors?

MR. NIEHAUS: I think that presents a different—

JUSTICE WHITE: He could say, "Well, the history of the death penalty in this community is such that there is prejudice against blacks, there is prejudice against blacks especially if they kill a white, and so I think that whites—there is a reasonable possibility that whites on this jury will be prejudiced against this defendant, and that is why—so I am going to strike all the whites I can strictly on a racial basis, assuming that—not assuming, but I think that they will be prejudiced against my clients." Now, what about that?

MR. NIEHAUS: Well, the harm is there, perhaps, but maybe not as severe, because in most areas of the country, I believe that even if a defendant exercises all of his challenges, he will not succeed in eradicating all white persons from the jury.

JUSTICE WHITE: But nevertheless, as you answered Justice [William J.] Brennan a while ago, you think it is the reason that is bad, the reason for striking, so that would be a racial reason for striking a white.

MR. NIEHAUS: Yes.

JUSTICE WHITE: And you say, but that is permissible.

MR. NIEHAUS: I think that it is not as serious a problem.

JUSTICE WHITE: That isn't what I asked you. Would that be constitutionally permissible or not?

MR. NIEHAUS: Pardon?

JUSTICE WHITE: Would that be constitutionally permissible, to strike the whites because of the—

JUSTICE STEVENS: What would be the constitutional basis for the claim that it was not permissible? What restricts a defendant from striking anybody once, or saying, "I don't like blacks," or "I don't like Jews," or whatever he wants to say? There is no state action involved here.

MR. NIEHAUS: I think that is exactly the point, that there is no state action involved where the defendant is exercising his peremptory challenge.

JUSTICE O'CONNOR: But there might be under an equal protection challenge if it is the state system that allows that kind of a strike.

MR. NIEHAUS: I believe that is possible. I am really not prepared to answer that specific question, but the idea of the Bill of Rights is to afford protection to the specific defendant.[5]

As Powell was contemplating how the case would be decided, these questions were fundamental, as evidenced by the fact that he wrote about this exchange in his oral argument notes.[6] Ironically, Niehaus seemed not to recognize the opportunity to win the case based on O'Connor's line of questioning. In fact, he readily admitted that he was not prepared to answer a question that could help him win the case. Niehaus's confusion was not lost on Justice Blackmun. In his own oral argument notes (figure 11), Blackmun wrote in green pencil five lines below Niehaus's name, "He quibbles on [positive questions]."

Powell's and Blackmun's notes certainly indicate that they picked up on an issue that was a potential turning point in *Batson*. But would it play a key role as the justices crafted the final opinion on the merits? Given that Powell ultimately wrote the majority opinion, such an effect seems plausible. Indeed, an analysis of the memos exchanged during the opinion-writing process suggests a strong relationship between what Powell learned about White's position and how Powell built a majority coalition.[7] Figure 12 shows Powell wondered whether he had accurately reflected White's views on the extent to which *Swain* should be overruled. Powell concluded the note by suggesting that he and White shared common ground in deciding the case.

After preparing a first draft of the majority opinion, Powell sent it privately to White in an effort to gauge his reaction. As figure 13 shows, White felt that Powell's draft was harder on *Swain* than necessary. However, he was not too upset with this result. In fact, he told Powell to circulate the draft and indicated that he would, at a minimum, concur in the result.

The following day, Powell sent a memo back to White explaining that the draft he circulated "made a number of changes that I hope will satisfy the concerns that you expressed." This memo (figure 14), highlights how the revised draft now emphasized "significant developments since *Swain* that lead us to reexamine its holding." In so doing, Powell provided White

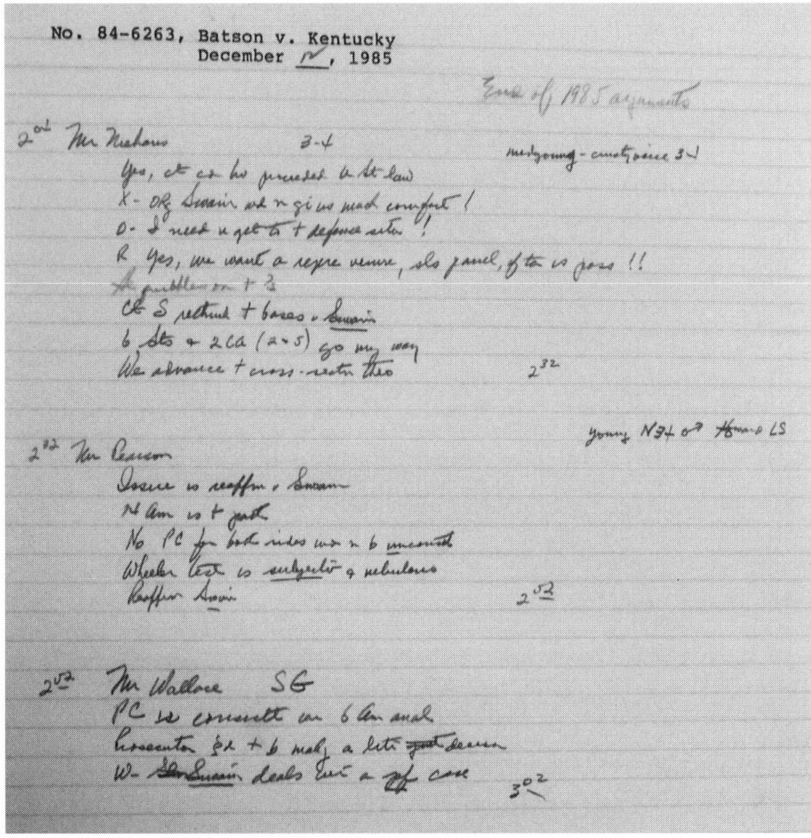

No. 84-6263, Batson v. Kentucky
December ___, 1985

Fig. 11. Justice Blackmun's notes from *Batson v. Kentucky.*
(A color reproduction of these notes can be found via the link at http://www.press.umich.edu/titleDetailDesc.do?id=4599894.)

a viable reason to join the majority opinion without feeling bound to the opinion he had written more than twenty years earlier. Powell concluded by noting that he would have joined White's *Swain* opinion had he been a member of the Court at the time. Powell's effort served two purposes. First, it let White know that Powell believed White had not taken an incorrect view of the case or the law when he wrote *Swain*. Second, it demonstrated that Powell believed that White could readily be a member of both majority opinions, alleviating any cognitive dissonance that might arise from a need to be consistent.

On January 31, White circulated a memo saying he would "likely join"

December 20, 1985

84-6263 Batson v. Kentucky

Dear Byron:

As the Chief has now assigned this case to me, I am particularly interested in your views as the author of Swain as to how an opinion should be written.

I enclose a copy of my Conference notes recording my understanding of your position. I believe you can read the notes despite poor handwriting and bad grammar. Do these accurately reflect the substance of what you said - though at greater length? I appreciate, of course, that how these views are written out will be what counts.

You may recall that I asked to what extent you think Swain must be overruled. It would be helpful if you also would share your thinking on this with me.

I recorded in my own notes the following:

"As I understand BRW, I think I could agree."

In short, I was with you.

Sincerely,

Justice White

lfp/ss

Fig. 12. Justice Powell's memo to Justice White, December 20, 1985, *Batson v. Kentucky*

Supreme Court of the United States
Washington, D. C. 20543

CHAMBERS OF
JUSTICE BYRON R. WHITE

January 21, 1986

84-6263 - Batson v. Kentucky

Dear Lewis,

Your draft is somewhat harder on Swain than it need be since it in effect finds that the decision was indefensible at the time in light of prior decisions. But perhaps this is just a matter of style. You should circulate, and I shall at least concur in the result.

Sincerely yours,

Byron

Justice Powell

Fig. 13. Justice White's response to Justice Powell's draft

January 22, 1986

84-6263 Batson v. Kentucky

Dear Byron:

In the draft I am circulating today, I have made a number of changes that I hope will satisfy the concerns that you expressed.

In particular, I have eliminated in appropriate places citations to decisions prior to Swain. Similarly - particularly in footnote 15 - I have eliminated citations to a number of the articles discussing Swain. Moreover, I have shown in textual changes that there have been significant developments since Swain that lead us to reexamine its holding. With these changes, I am circulating my opinion today.

If you have suggestions for changes in language, I will certainly consider them. If I had been a member of the Court when Swain was decided, I would have joined your opinion.

Sincerely,

Justice White

lfp/ss

Fig. 14. Justice Powell's memo indicating changes

Powell's draft. White eventually did so, but he also wrote a concurrence explaining his views on why he agreed with the Court's overturning of the principal holding in *Swain*. The Court ultimately decided in favor of Batson and reversed the Kentucky Supreme Court's decision.[8]

Batson raises a number of questions. Is the conversation at oral argument, along with the private communications, systematically prevalent in other cases? In other words, do justices systematically take note of what other justices say during oral argument? If so, what explains that process?

Moreover, if there are systematic explanations for the justices' note taking, how do they affect the coalition-formation process when, after conference, they exchange memos indicating their reaction to majority draft opinions? In this chapter, we seek answers to these questions.

To obtain such answers, we first formulate a theory of how justices use oral arguments to learn about their colleagues' preferences, integrating insights from social psychology, game theoretic information models, and the median voter model to generate hypotheses about to whom the justices listen at oral arguments. From there, we discuss data we use to test these hypotheses based on the entire collection of Powell's and Blackmun's oral argument notes. We then present the results of our analysis before turning to a test of whether learning colleagues' preferences at oral argument affects how justices interact with one another while bargaining and accommodating each other during the opinion-writing stage of the decision-making process.

Coordinating during Oral Arguments

As we noted in chapter 1, prior research has not specified what happens in the interim between oral arguments and the final voting coalition. That is, what mechanism (or mechanisms) leads justices to join final coalitions based on what transpires during these proceedings? We seek to provide such an explanation by tying the conversations that transpire during oral arguments to the opinion-writing stage of the Court's decision-making process.

Specifically, we explicate three hypotheses for how justices may use oral arguments to coordinate with one another. Initially, we argue that if actors have similar preferences regarding outcomes, cheap talk signals may help them coordinate (Johnson 2004). As Lupia and McCubbins (1998, 50) explain, "[P]ersuasion does not occur if the principal believes that the speaker is likely to have conflicting interests. If, however, the principal believes that common interests are more likely, then persuasion is possible." Thus, cheap talk allows coordination between actors with similar preferences because it is inherently easier for them to agree than it is for actors with divergent views to do so. For example, Morrow (1994, 256) notes that legislative debate "provides a way for legislators with similar underlying preferences to coordinate their votes" because "[m]embers are unlikely to take cues from those whose underlying values are greatly different from their own." More generally, scholars demonstrate that, theoretically and empirically, this is a necessary condition for actors to coordinate with another through cheap talk signals (Crawford and Sobel 1982; Farrell and Rabin 1996; Lupia and McCubbins 1998).

As justices interact with one another they must procure information about their colleagues' views concerning specific cases if the justices are to reach decisions that end up as close as possible to their preferred outcomes. While existing literature indicates that many opportunities exist for justices to gather this information, including from agenda-setting votes in the present case (Caldeira, Wright, and Zorn 1999) and from past merits votes in similar cases (Maltzman, Spriggs, and Wahlbeck 2000), oral arguments also provide an important forum for doing so. To see why, we consider oral arguments as a forum where questions and comments may signal a justice's preferences to the rest of the Court. More specifically, justices often use these proceedings to help coordinate with their ideological allies about the final policy outcomes.[9]

A brief example highlights this point. In *Bowsher v. Synar* (1986), the Court addressed the separation of powers when it voted 7–2 to strike down the Balanced Budget and Emergency Deficit Control Act, which represented an attempt by Congress to control the federal deficit by imposing automatic budget cuts. The cuts were to be overseen by the comptroller general, who was a member of the legislative branch. The Court ruled that the Constitution permitted laws to be enforced only by executive branch members and not by legislative branch members, who can only be removed by the legislative branch itself. Thus, the Court reasoned, Congress effectively retained control over the execution of the act itself and intruded into an executive function.

Powell took seven pages of notes during oral arguments on the case. On the bottom of the last page of his notes, he wrote in the margin "Note," along with an arrow pointing to the words, "C.J. said the C[omptroller] G[eneral]'s functions always have been performed by Congress."[10] This argument served as the foundation of the majority opinion that Burger wrote and Powell joined. More important for our argument here, Burger was ideologically proximate to Powell during the 1985 term. Thus, we hypothesize:

> *Hypothesis 1:* Justices use oral arguments to gather information from those who are ideologically close to them.

Beyond what we learn from cheap talk theory, we turn to insights from social psychology on the role of information in persuasive communications. Albarracin (2002) offers a multistage theoretical model of information interpretation, selection, and usage. Most relevant for our purposes is the third stage of her model, where an individual selects which information to use in decision making. Albarracin suggests that "individuals retrieve information from prior knowledge primarily to validate or refute information they receive" (68). While the first part of this argument lends credence to Hypothesis 1, we are also interested in information that directly refutes a justice's personal desired legal policy outcomes.

It seems straightforward that justices would seek information that directly supports their preferred policy outcomes, but it may seem counterintuitive that they would want information that opposes their preferred policy. However, we posit that justices desire information that directly refutes a preferred policy outcome because it enables them to better prepare counterarguments against ideological foes when building coalitions after oral arguments.[11] Hence, to the extent that justices' ideology drives their preferences regarding legal policy, we expect them to pay attention to their distant opponents at the same time that they listen to their allies.

Blackmun often gathered information about positions opposite to his own; *Gravel v. United States* (1972) provides a nice illustration. In this case, the Court found itself immersed in matters of national security when Senator Mike Gravel, chair of the Subcommittee on Buildings and Grounds, read out loud portions of the classified Pentagon Papers at a public committee meeting and later introduced the full papers into the *Senate Record.* Gravel also arranged to have Beacon Press publish the papers. The ensuing investigation by the Justice Department attempted to interrogate one of Gravel's aides, Leonard Rodberg, in hopes of ascertaining how Gravel and his staff obtained the papers. Gravel and Rodberg eventually filed suit, claiming the investigation violated the Speech and Debate Clause because such protection extends to congressional aides.

At oral argument, Blackmun took a page and a half of notes about the positions presented by counsel as well as about what some of his colleagues had to say. In particular, he made references to two of his more liberal colleagues, Justices Brennan and William O. Douglas. On the first page, he noted, "D[ouglas]—can you steal from the public domain?" On the second page, he noted, "Br[ennan]—Do not our opinions emphasize info to the people as the *purpose* of speech and debate."[12] These notes are interesting for two reasons. First, Brennan and Douglas were ideologically distant from Blackmun. Indeed, this case was heard early in Blackmun's career, when he was still relatively conservative and essentially opposed Brennan's and Douglas's views.[13]

Second, both Brennan and Douglas wrote dissents in *Gravel* while Blackmun joined White's majority opinion.[14] Specifically, in his dissent, Douglas argued that the Speech and Debate Clause should shield Beacon Press from any inquiry because the Pentagon Papers were put into the public domain through the subcommittee record. This was the same objection that Blackmun had noted that Douglas raised during oral argument. Further, Brennan posited in dissent that the majority restricted speech and debate, which endangered legislative tasks "vital to the workings of our democratic system" (dissent, 648). The majority directly countered both of these arguments. It held that immunity did not extend to the senator's aide testifying before the grand jury about the alleged arrangement for private publication (Douglas's argument) because there was no connection with the legislative process. In addition, the majority countered Brennan's argument, suggesting that the aide's immunity extended only to legislative acts to which the senator would be immune. In short, Blackmun noted the key issues for Brennan and Douglas that would become focal points in their dissents, and the majority opinion responded to these issues. Accordingly, we posit:

> *Hypothesis 2:* Justices use oral arguments to gather information from those who are ideologically farthest from them.

Finally, we turn to the role of the median justice, who is typically viewed as essential for the formation of a majority coalition (Murphy 1964). This view stems from the median voter model (e.g., Downs 1957), which states that in a unidimensional policy space all actors can be arranged according to their preferences, and the median voter will control the winning coalition (i.e., the winning coalition must contain the median voter, assuming single-peaked preferences). The typical median voter model assumes that actors have complete information, which implies that oral arguments may not matter for how the Court decides. However, our application of this model is premised on the idea that justices have incomplete information about the views of their colleagues and the case before them. Hence, any information a justice can learn about the median justice or justices close to the median, as well as information about the case and relevant law, is valuable. Conversely, justices further from the median are less relevant in terms of controlling the likely opinion coalitions. In sum, the further justices are from the median, the less valued their comments become.

Several examples illustrate the importance of the median justice. During oral arguments in *Super Tire Engineering Company v. McCorkle* (1974), a case that determined the eligibility of striking union workers for public assistance and welfare benefits, Blackmun notes comments made by the median, White, four separate times.[15] In *Buffalo Forge Co. v. Steelworkers* (1976), both Blackmun and Powell note separate questions from the term median, White, who ultimately ended up writing the majority opinion. Blackmun notes White's question to the respondent, whom Blackmun ultimately supported, while Powell notes White's questions to the petitioner, whom Powell supported.[16] During oral arguments in *Arnett v. Kennedy* (1974), which addressed whether the federal government may dismiss a nonprobationary employee without a preremoval hearing, Powell notes a comment made by White (the median during the 1973 term) as well as two comments by Potter Stewart, whose Martin-Quinn ideal point placed him extremely close to the median (0.12 units away), and one comment by Rehnquist, who went on to write the plurality opinion that was joined by Stewart and in which Powell concurred in part.[17] In another case, *United States v. Larionoff* (1977), Blackmun notes three comments by White, who was extremely close to the median (Stewart was the median that term, 0.16 units away from White).[18] This leads us to hypothesize:

> *Hypothesis 3:* Justices use oral arguments to assess the policy preferences of colleagues who are closer to the median more often than other justices.

Data and Methods

To test our hypotheses, we use two unique data sets consisting of all the notes taken by Blackmun and Powell during oral arguments. For Blackmun, these notes span the start of the 1970 term through the 1993 term. For Powell, the notes extend from January 1972 through the 1986 term. These notes are significant because they provide an explicit measure of learning for Blackmun and Powell. In other words, we assume that when they wrote down a colleague's question or comment, Blackmun and Powell believed that they could learn something about that colleague's preferences about how to decide a case. Furthermore, we assume that when they wrote down information about the case, they were learning something they did not already know. In turn, we posit that Blackmun and Powell used this knowledge to determine how the coalition-formation process would play out—either in terms of helping them build a majority coalition by learning what it would take to convince others to join opinions they wrote, or in terms of helping them better understand the boundaries of a case and the opposition's arguments that might arise during the coalition-formation process.

We derive our dependent variable by coding all of Blackmun and Powell's oral argument notes. Doing so allows us to determine the types of information they recorded and whether they attributed what was said to one of their colleagues. The data set includes an observation for each justice in every case in the sample because these two justices had the potential to write down something said by the other eight justices with whom they served. Our sample therefore includes 22,559 observations across 2,890 cases for Blackmun and 12,666 observations across 1,832 cases for Powell. The dependent variable, then, is a count of the total number of notations made by Blackmun or Powell about something one of their colleagues said.

To be precise about how we derive our dependent variable, figures 15 and 16 provide examples from Blackmun and Powell's notes in two cases. Figure 15 depicts Blackmun's oral argument notes from *Patterson v. McLean Credit Union* (1989) and is a representative example of Blackmun's note-taking process. Blackmun usually used just one sheet per case, and each included the name and date of the case at the top; the first section is always the petitioner's argument. In *Patterson,* he began by noting the time and name of the petitioner's attorney. Below the attorney's name, he then took notes about the arguments made, including case facts and legal precedent, and he made references to comments or questions from other justices. Under the petitioner's section there are two references to Kennedy ("K").[19] Under the respondent's section, there are several more references to Scalia, Kennedy, and White. Thus, for this particular case in our data set, White received a two for total references to him, Kennedy received a three, and Scalia received a one. (We do not include the reference to Scalia, where Blackmun notes, "AS is trying to act neutral.") The other five justices (O'Connor, Rehnquist, Brennan, Marshall, and Stevens) are all coded as zero.

Several other features of Blackmun's notes are important to fully grasp the nuances of what he observed during oral arguments. For example, the numbers or letters directly to the right of each attorney's name are grades assigned by Blackmun and are a measure of the quality of argument they provided (Johnson, Wahlbeck, and Spriggs 2006). Second, to the far right of Kaplan's name are some descriptive adjectives about the attorney's appearance ("short," "bald"), which we take as Blackmun's way of remembering who argued a case. Third, the lower left corner shows the initials of all the justices in two groups. These initials represent Blackmun's predictions about how his colleagues would vote in the case (see chapter 4).[20]

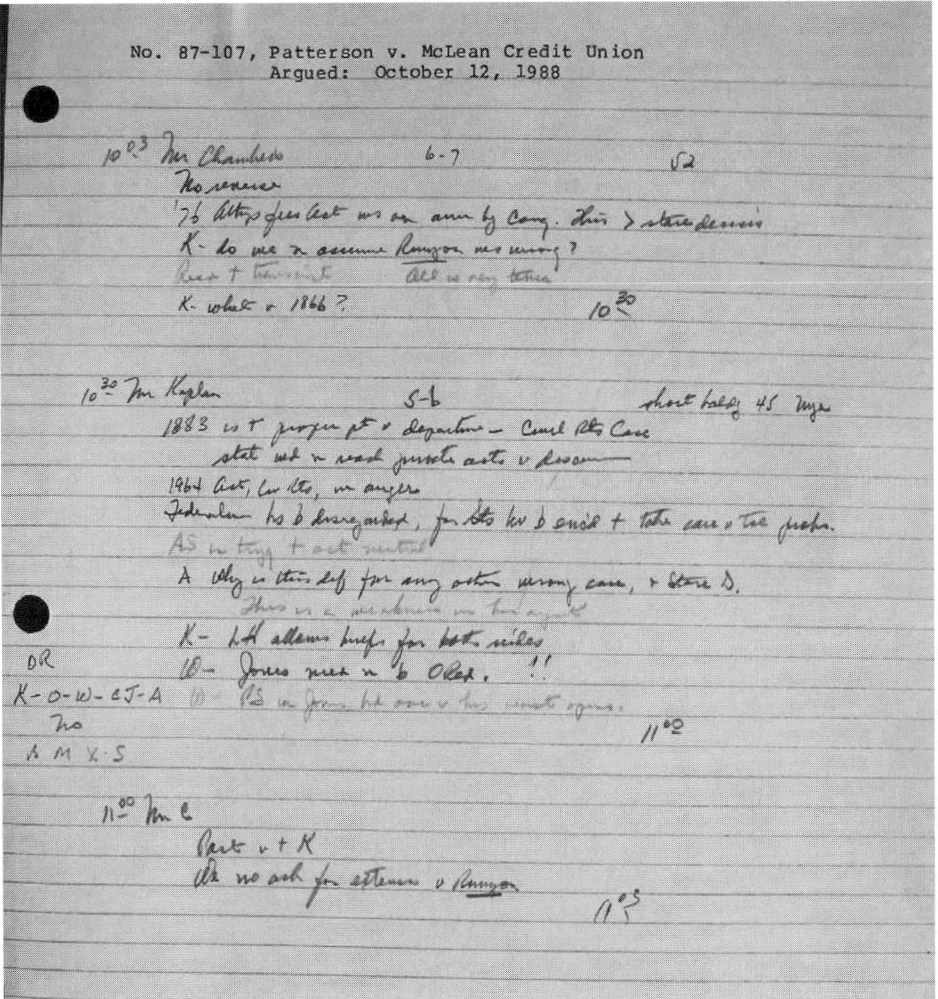

No. 87-107, Patterson v. McLean Credit Union
Argued: October 12, 1988

Fig. 15. Justice Blackmun's notes in *Patterson v. McLean Credit Union.*
(A color reproduction of these notes can be found via the link at http://www.press.umich.edu/titleDetailDesc.do?id=4599894.)

Figure 16 provides a similar example for Powell in *Pittsburgh Press v. Pittsburgh Commission* (1973). Powell took notes differently from Blackmun. First, Powell's notes occupied many more pages—in this case, four. The first page always has the case name, date, and docket number typed on top. Above his notes for the petitioner and respondent arguments, Powell would sometimes give his impressions of the case after the argu-

No. 72-419 PITTSBURG PRESS v. PITTSBURGH COMMISSION Argued 3/20/73

Very close case – await discussion at Conference

Bill Kelly's views:

Threshold Q: Relationship bet. law imposed on employers + that applicable to Press. Law is same – e.g. Press could designate "sex" where employers establish a reason for it.

Limited case: not dealing with editorial ads – e.g. someone stating his views. Also Press is free to reject any + all adds. (I'm not clear that Bill is right – except in degree – as to distinction bet. ed. ads + want ads.)

Volk (for Pittsburg Press)

Male Interest – Female Interest – Male/Female also large Box – disclaimer

Advertiser's preference will be honored, but in absence of preference newspaper makes decision. Though, almost always the judgment is in the end made by advertiser.

Newspaper does make a general editorial judgment as to needs of readers – employees & prospective employees. It is an editorial judgment that this is a sound service, helpful to all concerned. It permits maximum response to an add.

If employer wants over the road truck drivers, a lot of time + money would be wasted if these ads are forbidden.

Volk said this case involves ads placed by employers – when preference is honored. Policy is different as to ads by persons seeking employment. The EEC would object to categorizing latter as to sex.

Papers do exercise discretion as to ads. Recently rejected Massage Parlor ad

The limited "occupational exceptions" are extremely limited.

Volk (cont)

First Amend. Rts should be extended to commercial advertising. Distinguishes Valentine – which is a hazy & wavering line.

Sullivan, Grosjean etc severely limit Valentine

If all of simplistic language in Valentine prevails – i.e. if we still accept this – Volk admits he loses.

But J. White suggests that it can be argued that even if Valentine is not restricted, the type of adds in this case are not commercials.

Help wanted adds are an editorial function in sense of a judgment as to what best serves public. How one arranges + make-up paper is an editorial function.

Government agencies – enforcing the host of new laws & regulations – should not impair freedom of press as a means of enforcing these laws & regulations – however meritorious

Court below said newspaper must "divine" the intent of advertisers

Strassburger (Pitt. Human Rel. Comm)

Sec 8 of Ordinance controls.

Two Const Qs.

I First Amend issue

Const. protection of speech is not absolute

Conduct is not protected.

Commercial advertising not protected (Valentine)

In Sullivan, ad was political – not commercial.

? | Economic interests (production of goods + services) are not protected by 1st Amend. [What about

Matson (Nat. Org. for Women)

Nothing helpful.

Fig. 16. Justice Powell's notes in *Pittsburgh Press v. Pittsburgh Commission*. (A color reproduction of these notes can be found via the link at http://www.press.umich.edu/titleDetailDesc.do?id=4599894.)

ments were done. Here he noted, "Very close case—await conference discussion." In this instance, Powell wrote only one comment made by a colleague—a reference to White on page 3. Thus, White receives a one for our dependent variable, and all other justices receive zeroes.[21]

Because our dependent variable is a count of the total notes Blackmun or Powell took about their colleagues' comments, we cannot use traditional linear regression: As Long (1997, 217) points out, "The use of [linear regression] models for count outcomes can result in inefficient, inconsistent, and biased estimates." Thus, we employ a more appropriate model, the negative binomial regression, which accounts for the positive contagion in our dependent variable (Long and Freese 2006, 349).[22]

The model contains several independent variables to test our three hypotheses. To test the first two hypotheses, we invoke ideal point estimates from Martin and Quinn (2002) to measure (in absolute value) each justice's ideological distance from Powell or Blackmun. Because we theorize that Powell and Blackmun may note comments from both their closest allies and their most distant opponents, we include both the absolute value and the absolute value squared (i.e., ideological distance and ideological distance squared). This approach allows ideological distance to have a curvilinear effect along the range of values. To test the hypothesis that Powell and Blackmun are more concerned with questions raised by the median justice (or by those justices close to the median), we also include a variable that measures the absolute distance of each of their colleagues from each term's median using Martin-Quinn scores (i.e., speaker's ideological distance from median).

Beyond our variables of interest, we also include several controls to capture alternative explanations for Powell's and Blackmun's behavior.[23] Because the chief justice has agenda-setting power at conference (Johnson, Spriggs, and Wahlbeck 2005; Wahlbeck 2006), a justice may be more interested in the chief's views during oral argument. Thus, we include *Speaker Was Chief Justice,* which is a dummy variable coded one for the chief and zero for all associate justices. In addition, justices may be more inclined to listen to a colleague who is relatively new because they may not know as much about his or her preferences. For example, Biskupic (2006) suggests that during the 2006 term, Roberts and Alito were relatively new to the Court, so the other justices were more likely to use oral arguments to get a sense of the two men's positions. In contrast, justices have much less need to make notes about colleagues with whom they have sat for more than a decade because they can draw on the colleagues' past behavior to infer their likely views. Accordingly, we include *Length of Joint Ser-*

vice, which is a variable coded as the total number of years that either Blackmun or Powell served with each of their colleagues.

Maltzman, Spriggs, and Wahlbeck (2000) demonstrate that issue experts often play an integral role in how decisions are made. Rather than a direct measure of experience, however, we are interested in a justice's expertise relative to Blackmun or Powell. To capture this concept, we first coded the percentage of cases within an issue area where one of these two wrote an opinion. This percentage is a rolling number that includes all decisions up to but not including the case specifically before the Court. *Issue Area Expertise,* the variable we employ, is measured by subtracting each recording justice's colleague's percentage from the percentage of the recording justice. Hence, large numbers indicate that a recording justice's colleague has more issue expertise, while small numbers indicate that the recording justice has more issue expertise.

We also control for whether a justice is more inclined to listen to colleagues in difficult cases. Specifically, we suspect that all else equal, justices should be more likely to listen to their colleagues as the number of available issues to consider—and potentially on which to decide the case—rises. We follow the recent insights of Collins (2008a, b) and measure complexity as the number of amicus briefs submitted in a case. This variable is labeled *Case Complexity.* In our data, the average case has roughly seven briefs submitted, with a standard deviation of approximately nine briefs.

Finally, we control for a factor directly relating to the courtroom structure. Johnson (2004) suggests that Powell was more inclined to note questions asked by justices who sat nearest to him during oral arguments. The logic is that even though the Court uses microphones during these proceedings, justices may find it easier to hear questions asked by those who sit directly next to them than by those who sit farther away. To determine the seating order on the bench, we utilize the portraits of the Court for each natural Court in the sample. This variable (*Physical Distance between Justices*), takes on a value of one for justices who sit directly next to Blackmun or Powell, two for those who sit in the next seats, and so on through the justice farthest from Blackmun or Powell, who is coded eight. We expect this variable to be negatively related to whether Blackmun or Powell notes a colleague's comments.

Results

Table 2 provides the results of our analysis about to whom Blackmun and Powell listen during oral arguments. Our first two hypotheses held that

Powell and Blackmun would listen to those closest to them ideologically as well as to those farthest away. These hypotheses stemmed from our theory that colleagues in these two categories would be most likely to provide the two justices with information that could later be used to support or refute their preferences and help them reach a desired policy outcome that garnered at least four other votes. The results from table 2 support our hypotheses, but it is also clear that each justice relies on information from different sources. To further demonstrate this result, we turn to predicted values calculated from our models.

Figure 17 depicts the predicted values for our ideological distance variable. The x-axis is the ideological distance between Blackmun (left panel) or Powell (right panel) and a colleague. The y-axis represents the expected number of references these two justices would record for a colleague in a single case, conditional on a particular value of ideological distance between the recording justice and his colleague.[24]

Evidently, while both justices use the arguments to learn about their

TABLE 2. Explaining the Total Number of References Made to Colleagues' Questions and Comments

	Blackmun	Powell
Ideological Distance	–0.071*	–0.288*
	(0.034)	(0.118)
Ideological Distance Squared	0.022*	–0.009
	(0.005)	(0.009)
Speaker's Ideological Distance from Median	–0.304*	–0.048
	(0.020)	(0.111)
Speaker Was Chief Justice	–0.083	–1.146*
	(0.056)	(0.146)
Length of Joint Service	–0.013*	–0.169*
	(0.003)	(0.008)
Issue Area Expertise	–0.012*	–0.009*
	(0.002)	(0.004)
Case Complexity	0.015*	–0.021*
	(0.004)	(0.011)
Physical Distance between Justices	–0.152*	–0.026
	(0.011)	(0.017)
Constant	–1.062*	–0.441*
	(0.059)	(0.098)
ln(α)	0.308*	1.143*
	(0.074)	(0.090)
Observations	22,559	12,666

Note: Negative binomial regression model of number of references made by Blackmun and Powell to their colleagues during oral arguments.

*denotes $p < 0.05$ (two-tailed test). Robust standard errors reported in parentheses.

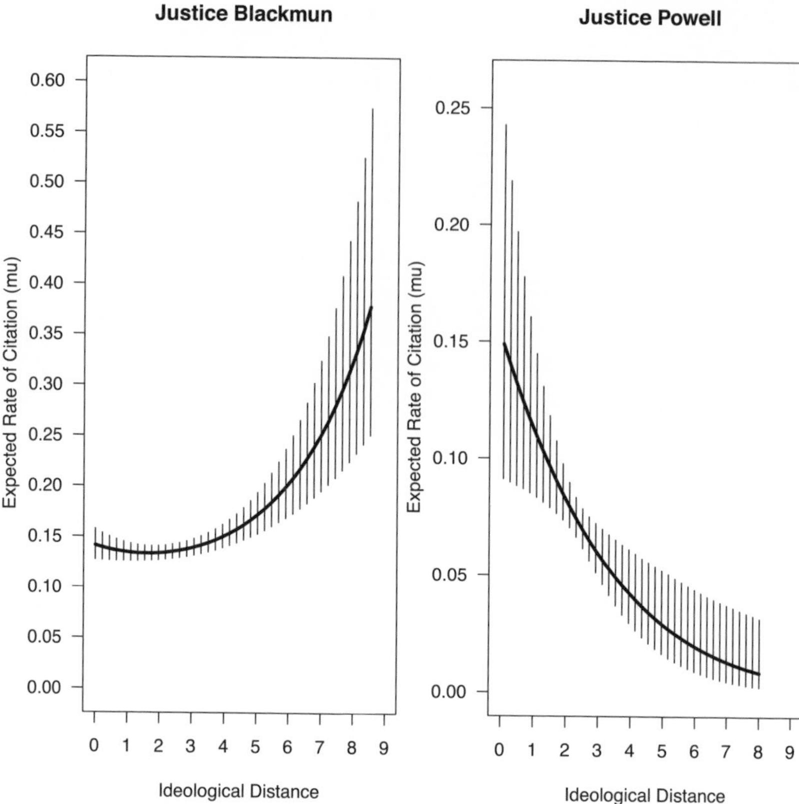

Fig. 17. Predicted probability of a justice referencing a colleague, by ideological distance. Effect of ideological distance between a speaking and a recording justice on the recording justice's (i.e., Blackmun's or Powell's) note citation rate. Vertical line segments denote 95 percent confidence intervals. All other variables were held at their modal or mean values, as appropriate. Point estimates and confidence intervals were obtained through stochastic simulations similar to Clarify.

colleagues, they listen to different groups. We focus first on Blackmun, who seems to use oral arguments to learn about ideologically distant colleagues. Indeed, when he is ideologically proximate to a colleague, we estimate that he will note a colleague once every seven cases. By contrast, when a colleague is distant from Blackmun, the citation rate increases by a factor of almost three (i.e., more than once every three cases).

This finding supports our second hypothesis and is intuitive for two reasons. First, as we posit, Blackmun seems to use oral arguments to determine what his ideological adversaries think about how they plan to decide a case in an effort to create counterarguments he may make when crafting or joining a majority argument. Second, listening to colleagues ideologically further from him allows Blackmun to begin thinking about the bounds of a decision if a distant coalition garners enough votes for a majority. As a result, listening to colleagues further away is innate, and Blackmun does so. Indeed, these arguments are consistent with the notes in figure 11 (*Batson*), where Blackmun wrote down what Rehnquist and O'Connor (two of the more conservative justices on the Court at that time) said.[25] These arguments are also consistent with figure 15 (his *Patterson* notes), where he focused on comments by Scalia and Kennedy.

While still using oral arguments as a mechanism for learning, Powell acts differently. When he and a colleague are ideologically close, we estimate that he would take note of a colleague's comment or question at roughly the same baseline rate as Blackmun—about once in every seven cases. However, whereas Blackmun becomes more likely to take note of something said by a colleague as ideological distance increases, we find the opposite effect for Powell. When the distance between Powell and a colleague reaches its observed maximum, the expected citation rate drops to less than one citation per more than one hundred cases.

This finding supports Hypothesis 1, that some justices listen to those colleagues who are most likely to help them build a majority coalition. This, too, is intuitive behavior. Specifically, by listening closely to what ideological allies say at oral arguments, Powell is setting up a situation where if he crafts a majority or simply seeks to join a majority coalition, he will know what those close to him think. This knowledge can aid in the bargaining and accommodation process regarding the policy the majority will eventually set. Our discussion of Powell's behavior in *Bowsher* (where he noted what he believed to be Burger's key focus in the case) supports these systematic findings.

Although Blackmun and Powell focused on different types of colleagues, their behavior suggests that they sought to determine how coalitions would begin to form after oral arguments. One justice in particular is most important for both men—the median. Indeed, as we hypothesize, the median is generally needed for a majority to form. However, we find mixed support for this hypothesis. Again we turn first to Blackmun. Figure 18 shows a strong effect; when a justice is close to (or is) the median, we expect Blackmun to take note of a colleague's statement about once in every four cases. When a justice is ideologically distant (close to eight on the x-axis), however, this citation rate plummets to less than one citation

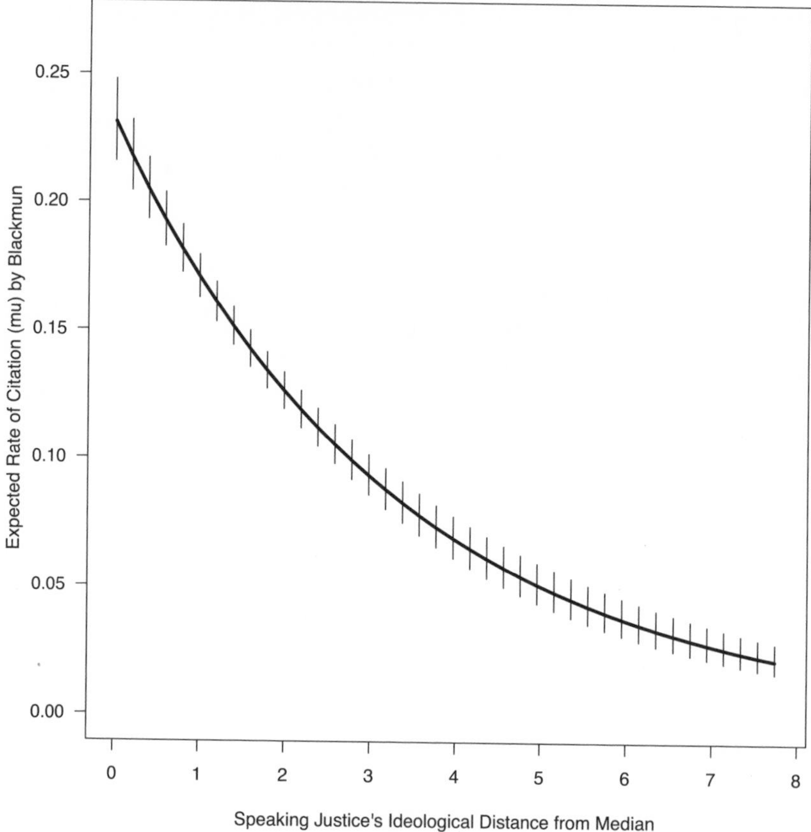

Fig. 18. Predicted probability of Justice Blackmun citing a colleague. Effect of a speaking justice's ideological distance from the median justice on Blackmun's note citation rate. We omit a panel for Powell as the variable is not statistically significant in his model ($p = 0.66$). Vertical line segments denote 95 percent confidence intervals. All other variables were held at their modal or mean values, as appropriate. Point estimates and confidence intervals were obtained through stochastic simulations similar to Clarify.

per twenty-plus cases. In short, Blackmun is more likely to listen to those close to the median. His behavior in *Batson* and *Patterson,* where he noted several comments and questions made by White (who was close to the median during these terms), supports this finding.

While Blackmun appears to be carefully attuned to the words of the median justice—and those close to him or her—our data suggest that this finding does not hold true for Powell. Indeed, we fail to find a systematic

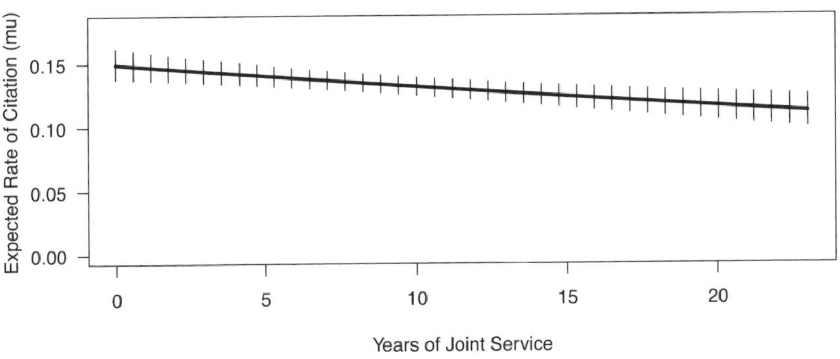

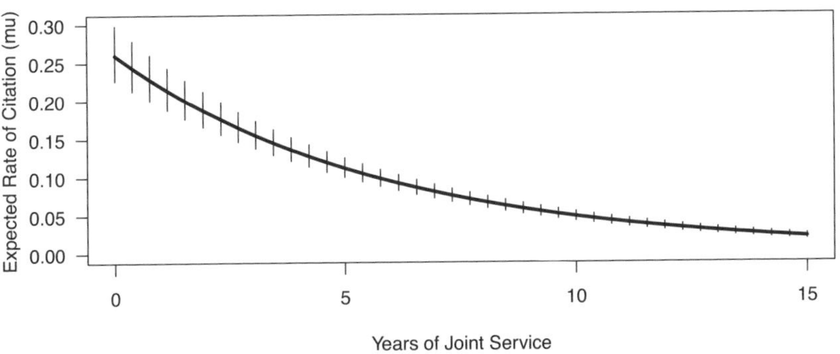

Fig. 19. Predicted probability of citing a colleague based on years of service. Effect of a speaking justice's number of years of joint service on the recording justice's (i.e., Blackmun's or Powell's) note citation rate. Vertical line segments denote 95 percent confidence intervals. All other variables were held at their modal or mean values, as appropriate. Point estimates and confidence intervals were obtained through stochastic simulations similar to Clarify.

relationship between Powell's notational behavior and the distance between a colleague and the median justice ($p = 0.66$).[26] While Powell and Blackmun listen to different colleagues, their overall behavior suggests that both justices use oral arguments to learn how their colleagues might act as they move toward a final opinion on the merits. This supports our general hypothesis about how justices utilize these proceedings.

Beyond our variables of interest that tap into justices' ideological relationships with one another, we also find that other factors systematically correspond with Blackmun and Powell's note-taking behavior during oral arguments. Figure 19 demonstrates that the length of joint service significantly affects both justices. The bottom panel shows that Powell takes one colleague-specific note in about every four cases when that colleague is a newcomer to the Court. As Powell learns more about his colleagues through joint service, however, the rate at which he takes notes drops off quickly, with the utterances of long-term colleagues exceedingly unlikely to motivate Powell to take notice.

While we also find a negative and statistically significant relationship for Blackmun (top panel), the magnitude of the relationship is clearly smaller, as evidenced by the more modest slope on Blackmun's line. Indeed, we estimate that Blackmun took note of an utterance by a freshman justice about once every seven cases. By contrast, when Blackmun has served with a colleague for more than twenty years, we estimate that his notation rate drops to about one reference in every nine cases.

The decrease in the expected citation rate for both justices suggests that a learning process is at work in which Powell and to a lesser extent Blackmun pay closer attention to what a new colleague says at oral argument. This result makes sense from the standpoint that Powell and Blackmun probably know less about the preferences held by those who are newest to the bench.

Figure 20 demonstrates that in their search for information to help them decide, Powell's and Blackmun's citation rates systematically correspond with the relative expertise of their colleagues in particular issue areas. When a justice is an expert relative to Blackmun or Powell (indicated by large negative numbers), both justices are significantly more likely to listen and note things the expert justice said. Specifically, for Blackmun, when listening to an issue area expert (–100), he takes note of a colleague's statement or question about twice every five cases, while Powell takes a note about half as often—that is, once every five cases. However, when Blackmun and Powell have much more expertise than the speaking justice, the expected rate of citation drops to about once in every ten cases for both justices. In short, these two justices demonstrate that they are willing to listen to colleagues believed to have expertise Powell and Blackmun do not share.

These results suggest that justice-specific characteristics affect Powell's and Blackmun's learning processes during oral arguments. At the case level, complexity (as measured by the number of amicus briefs filed) affects these two justices, but not in the same way. Figure 21 indicates that Blackmun is more likely to seek guidance from other justices when the potential number of issues in a case increases. The (albeit post hoc) intuition for us is that more amici add more issues to the record, and it is therefore

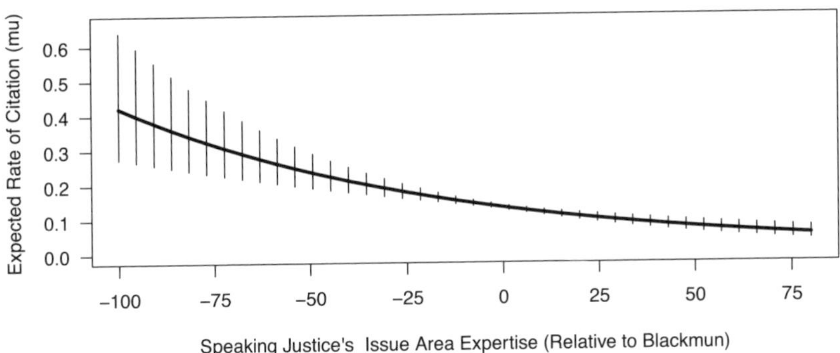

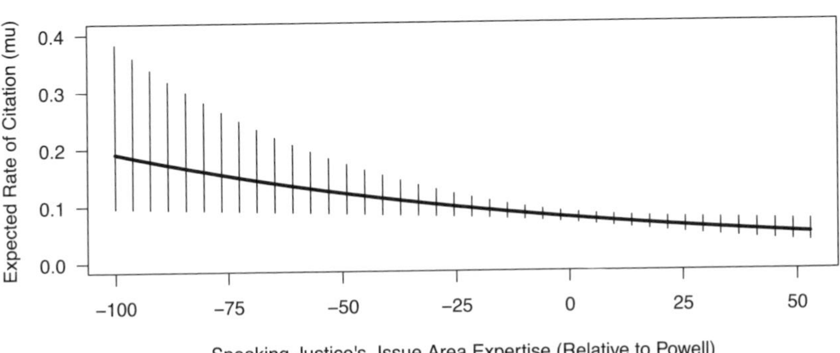

Fig. 20. Predicted probability of citing a colleague based on relative issue area expertise. Effect of a speaking justice's issue area expertise on the recording justice's (i.e., Blackmun's or Powell's) note citation rate. Large negative values indicate that the speaking justice had more expertise than the recording justice. Large positive values indicate the recording justice had more relative expertise than the speaking justice. Vertical line segments denote 95 percent confidence intervals. All other variables were held at their modal or mean values, as appropriate. Point estimates and confidence intervals were obtained through stochastic simulations similar to Clarify.

less clear which issues will eventually be the focus of the Court's decision. Conversely, Powell is less likely to seek guidance from other justices when complexity increases. The reason for this may be that Powell is simply focusing on how he thinks about a case and does not worry as much about his colleagues' views. Whatever the reason, though, the effect is not very large for either Blackmun or Powell.

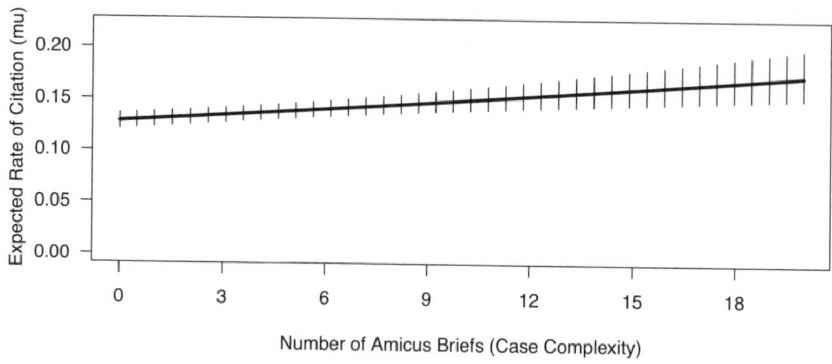

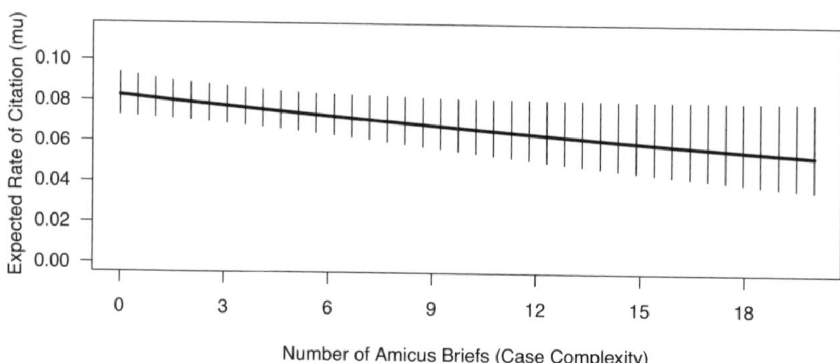

Fig. 21. Predicted probability of citing a colleague based on case complexity. Effect of the number of amicus briefs (i.e., case complexity) on the recording justice's (i.e., Blackmun's or Powell's) note citation rate. Vertical line segments denote 95 percent confidence intervals. All other variables were held at their modal or mean values, as appropriate. Point estimates and confidence intervals were obtained through stochastic simulations similar to Clarify.

Finally, we infer from figure 22 that even after controlling for ideological, justice-level, and case-level explanations, the physical environment of the courtroom affects Blackmun and Powell. While this may seem an odd argument, the acoustics of a large room seem to make it more difficult to hear colleagues who sit farther away during the proceedings. This is what we find. In particular, Powell is slightly less likely to make note of something said by the colleague sitting farthest away. The effect for Blackmun is much more pronounced; his expected notation rate plum-

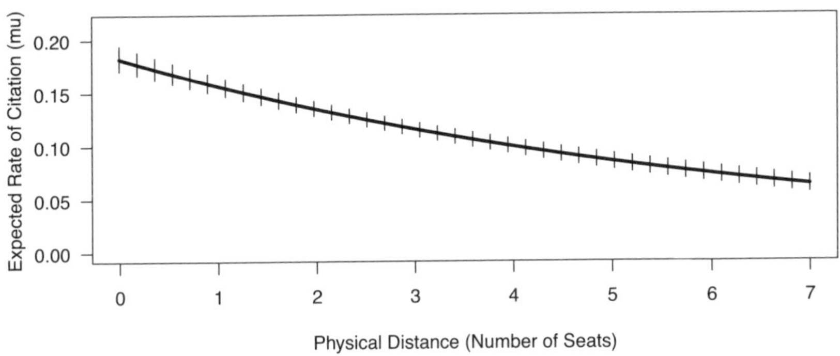

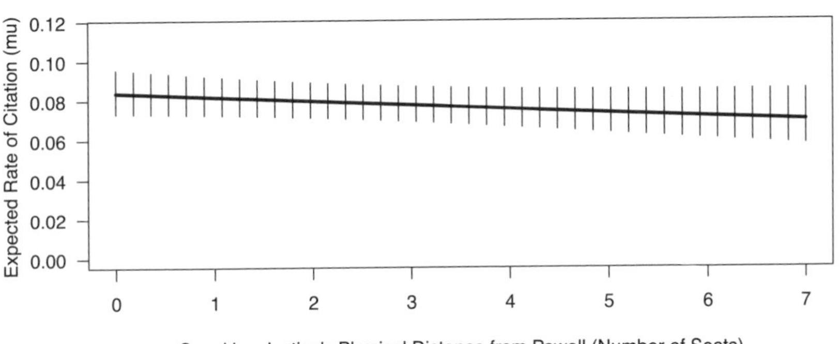

Fig. 22. Predicted probability of citing a colleague based on physical distance from justice. Effect of a speaking justice's physical distance from the recording justice's (i.e., Blackmun's or Powell's) note citation rate. Vertical line segments denote 95 percent confidence intervals. All other variables were held at their modal or mean values, as appropriate. Point estimates and confidence intervals were obtained through stochastic simulations similar to Clarify.

mets from about once in every five cases for the colleague seated next to him to about once in every twelve cases for the colleague farthest away.

Does Listening Matter?

This discussion and analysis provide an unparalleled view into the minds of two Supreme Court justices during a critical stage in the Court's decision-making process. Despite the fact that Blackmun and Powell use different approaches to note taking, we find a series of commonalities in their behavior as well as some important differences. We believe that these data dramatically enhance our collective understanding of the importance of oral arguments and how justices use these proceedings to gather information. But we readily acknowledge that this is only a single—though important—part of the overall story.

As our discussion of *Batson* illustrates, information from oral argument can—and often does—affect case outcomes and the content of the Court's opinions. Existing research provided by Johnson (2004) shows, for example, that Powell is more likely to join a final coalition on the merits with those to whom he listens more during oral arguments. In this section we move a step back in the process and examine how information gathered by Blackmun and Powell corresponds with their colleagues' behavior during the opinion-writing process. Specifically, we focus on how other justices interact with Blackmun and Powell when one of these two justices is writing the majority opinion. That is, conditional on having received a draft opinion authored by either of the two recording justices, how do their colleagues respond to these drafts?

Using data from the Burger Court Opinion Writing Database (Wahlbeck, Spriggs, and Maltzman 2009), we analyze the responses from Blackmun's and Powell's colleagues to the initial majority-opinion drafts they circulated while serving during the Burger Court. For Blackmun, this data set consists of 1,333 responses across 187 opinions. For Powell, the set consists of 1,080 responses across 167 draft opinions. In particular, we develop a nominal dependent variable that takes on one of the following values depending on how a colleague responded: (A) joins majority opinion, (B) makes a suggestion, (C) announces inclination (i.e., leaning) toward a separate opinion, or (D) joins a separate opinion.[27]

We include several independent variables that might help explain this process. First, we include *Number of Speaker References*, our dependent variable from the previous section. Recall that this variable is simply the number of justice-specific references Powell or Blackmun make in a case. Second, we include *Overall Amount of Oral Argument Notes*, which controls for the overall amount of information the two justices garner from oral arguments and is a count of the number of lines of notes written by each justice. Third, we control for the ideological distance between Blackmun or Powell and each of their colleagues in the same essential way we do in the previous model (i.e., *Ideological Distance*).[28] Finally, we include

TABLE 3. Oral Argument Notes and Coalition Formation

	Blackmun	Powell
Make Suggestion		
Number of Speaker References	–13.680*	–0.358
	(0.336)	(0.817)
Overall Amount of Oral Argument Notes	0.008	0.003
	(0.042)	(0.013)
Ideological Distance	–0.163	–0.403*
	(0.206)	(0.202)
Issue Area Expertise	–0.020*	–0.006
	(0.007)	(0.015)
Constant	–3.866*	–3.447*
	(0.472)	(0.510)
Lean toward Separate Opinion		
Number of Speaker References	–1.118	0.601
	(0.968)	(0.429)
Overall Amount of Oral Argument Notes	–0.021	0.005
	(0.020)	(0.006)
Ideological Distance	–0.131	–0.020
	(0.134)	(0.121)
Issue Area Expertise	–0.031*	0.032
	(0.011)	(0.024)
Constant	–3.042*	–3.943*
	(0.346)	(0.372)
Join Separate Opinion		
Number of Speaker References	0.493*	0.581*
	(0.160)	(0.183)
Overall Amount of Oral Argument Notes	–0.026*	–0.006
	(0.011)	(0.003)
Ideological Distance	0.135*	0.082*
	(0.040)	(0.042)
Issue Area Expertise	–0.015*	–0.010
	(0.005)	(0.007)
Constant	–1.247*	–1.167*
	(0.158)	(0.169)
Observations	1,333	1,080

Note: Multinomial logistic regression model of a justice's initial response to a draft majority opinion circulated by Blackmun and Powell. The baseline category is when a justice responds by joining the majority opinion.

*denotes $p < 0.05$ (two-tailed test). Robust standard errors reported in parentheses.

Issue Area Expertise, which is also measured in the same way as described in the previous model.

Because our dependent variable is nominal, we estimate two multinomial logistic regression models and report parameter estimates for these models in table 3.[29] Here, too, we focus primarily on visual interpretations of our results, which we provide in figures 23 and 24.

Figure 23 shows the effect of noting a reference made by a colleague and indicates that the responses to Blackmun's and Powell's majority-opinion drafts are very similar. Each graph contains four shaded regions that represent the probability of Blackmun and Powell receiving each type of response.[30] For example, when there are zero references to any given justice, the largest category (i.e., the most probable outcome) for both justices is to receive a "join majority" memo from the other justices. The second-largest category for both justices is to receive a "join separate" memo. The smallest two categories at the bottom of each graph, which are difficult to see as a consequence of their low probability, are receive a "make a suggestion" memo (represented by the thin white area) and receive a "lean separate" memo (represented by the thin black area).

As the panels from the figure make clear, we find that for both Blackmun and Powell, an increased number of notes about a colleague during oral argument is negatively related to that colleague's likelihood of joining a majority-opinion draft written by either justice. When Blackmun makes zero references to a particular colleague, the probability of that colleague joining a Blackmun-penned majority draft is over 0.70. However, when Blackmun notes four references for that colleague, the probability of that colleague joining a Blackmun-penned majority draft drops to approximately 0.35. In other words, as Blackmun makes more references to his colleagues, they are less likely to join his majority opinion and twice as likely to join a separate opinion. The substantive effect for opinions authored by Powell is nearly identical.

These findings suggest that Blackmun and Powell are less prone to listen to colleagues they believe are sure to join their opinions. Stated differently, their colleagues are more likely to join the two justices' draft opinions when they do not make any notations to those colleagues. This finding at first seems counterintuitive. However, it seems reasonable that Blackmun and Powell might be trying to make notations about justices who are not expected allies as a way of strengthening their coalitions. They might do so for a couple of different reasons. For example, because Powell notes colleagues who are ideologically close to him, he might be taking notes when he feels he has a chance to make a majority coalition stronger by trying to persuade another justice because of his or her close proxim-

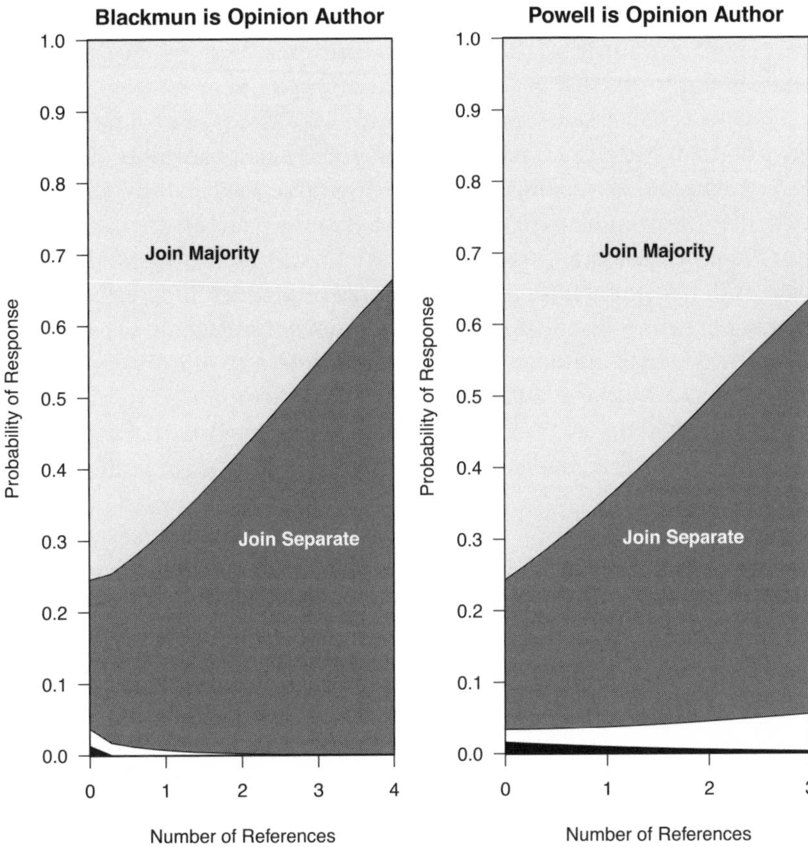

Fig. 23. Predicted probability of a justice's initial response to a circulated draft majority opinion, by number of references. Area plot of a justice's initial response to a majority opinion authored by Blackmun (*left panel*) and Powell (*right panel*), conditional on the number of references concerning that justice taken by Blackmun/Powell during oral arguments. The white and black areas at the bottom of each plot represent the probability that a justice responds by making a suggestion or leans toward joining a separate opinion, respectively. All other variables were held at their median values. We used the prgen command as implemented in SPost by Long and Freese (2006) to generate these values.

ity. Conversely, Blackmun's notations regarding ideologically distant justices suggests that he may be gathering that information to strengthen his majority opinion by preparing a better counterargument. Thus, while the justices appear not to be listening to other justices who might be sure joiners if Powell or Blackmun were to write the opinion, they are instead listening to those who may join a coalition in the hopes of persuading them

(Powell) or are likely listening to justices with opposing viewpoints to prepare counterarguments (Blackmun). In sum, these findings are consistent with the argument that coalition formation begins at oral argument.

Figure 24 illustrates a similar quantity—the effect of total number of lines of notes taken by each justice on his colleagues' probability of joining a draft opinion. Here, too, we find nearly identical substantive effects for both Blackmun and Powell (i.e., the shapes in the panel are the same). Unlike the previous figure, however, here we find a positive relationship between the amount of information harvested by a justice and the likelihood that a colleague joins the opinion draft. When both Blackmun and Powell take a very small number of notes, we estimate roughly a 25 percent chance that a colleague will opt to join a separate opinion. When Blackmun is an active note taker, however, and gathers a substantial amount of information during oral argument, the same likelihood plummets to around 10 percent.

These findings suggest that while they listen to different colleagues during oral arguments, Blackmun and Powell still use the information gleaned to increase the likelihood that others will join their draft majority opinions. For us, this finding is intuitive. Indeed, because Powell was often the median on the Court, he had an incentive to pay more attention to colleagues who were ideologically proximate to him on either side of the ideological divide because he needed to decide which coalition to join. Conversely, Blackmun was more of an ideologue (conservative in his early years and later liberal) and therefore needed to seek information to combat potential opposing coalitions. Moreover, our results show that learning at oral argument (i.e., gathering information about the law, case facts, and their colleagues) enables justices to be more effective coalition builders when writing majority opinions.

Conclusion

Here we have taken the next step toward understanding how Supreme Court justices may use oral arguments to begin their coalition-formation process. It is the first attempt to connect systematically oral arguments with the exchange of memos during the bargaining and accommodation stage that is crucial to the coalition-formation process. We theorized that justices would approach oral arguments with the goal of learning about the case and their colleagues' preferences.

Specifically, we contend that justices learn about their colleagues during these proceedings, but we are agnostic on exactly how they learn.

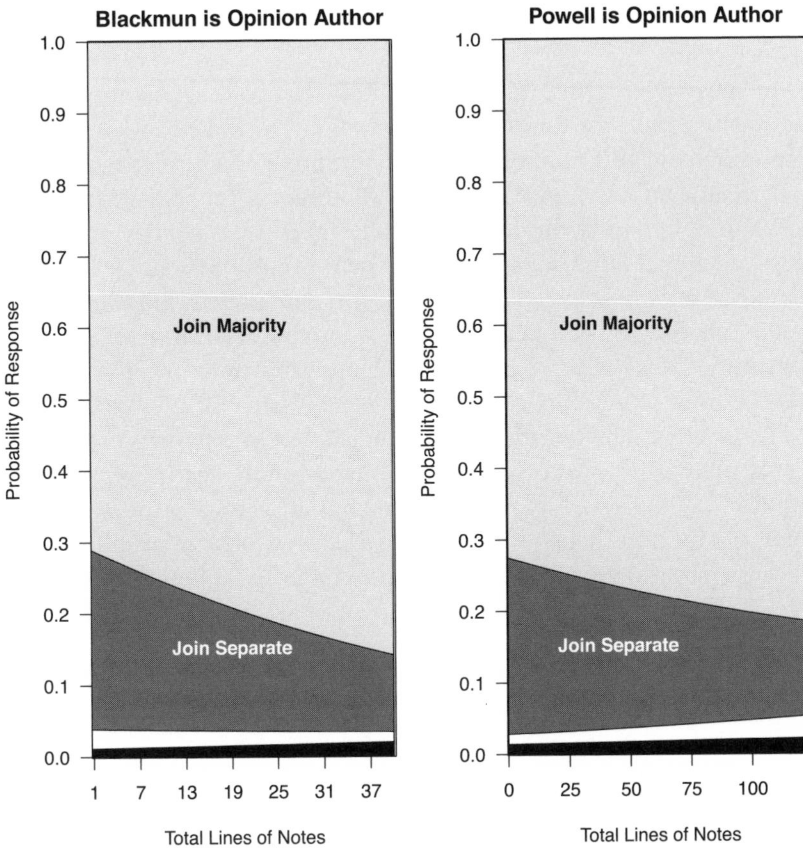

Fig. 24. Predicted probability of a justice's initial response to a circulated draft majority opinion, by total number of lines. Area plot of a justice's initial response to a majority opinion authored by Blackmun (*left panel*) and Powell (*right panel*), conditional on the amount of notes taken by Blackmun/Powell during oral arguments. The white and black areas at the bottom of each plot represent the probability that a justice responds by making a suggestion or leans toward joining a separate opinion, respectively. All other variables were held at their median values. We used the prgen command as implemented in SPost by Long and Freese (2006) to generate these values.

Blackmun seems to use the proceedings to determine where his potential adversaries may come down in the case, while Powell is more prone to listen to those with whom he may join a coalition. The justices exhibited a similar pattern of receiving responses from their colleagues based on the citations made to others and the total number of notes they take in a case. In both instances, however, interactions during the opinion-writing phase begin where we suspected—when attorneys try to make their arguments in open court.

In substantive terms, this chapter shows that oral arguments serve as the starting place for the coalition-formation process. But what are the implications of this finding? The evidence presented here suggests that oral arguments are of great importance and have great consequence. On occasion, as in *Batson,* the decisive legal theory emerges not from the brief of the petitioner but from a question raised at oral argument by a justice. Moreover, in *Batson,* one of O'Connor's questions directly followed previous questioning by colleagues who were looking for answers about the constitutional basis of hypothetical claims similar to the petitioner's stated claims.

Thus, this chapter demonstrates the connection between oral arguments and how the Court reaches an outcome on the merits. But is there another way to show that these proceedings are important to case outcomes? In the next chapter we attempt to do so by exploring how these proceedings may allow a justice to predict how his or her colleagues will act.

4 | Predicting Coalitions from Oral Arguments

Chapter 3 demonstrates that oral arguments are often a conversation among justices where they learn about colleagues' preferences by listening to each other's questions and comments. Further, what justices learn from these conversations corresponds to the bargaining and accommodation that take place as they hammer out their final legal and policy decisions during the opinion-writing process. While this finding suggests the overall utility of oral arguments in the formation and building of coalitions at the Court, it does not directly address a closely related question: whether justices can use oral arguments to build a road map of the likely coalitions that will emerge in a case.

Here, we continue examining the Burger Court era and specifically Justice Harry A. Blackmun, who kept explicit notes about the coalitions he expected to emerge in many of the cases he heard. Chapter 3 offered a glimpse of Blackmun's fortune-telling success when he correctly predicted all nine votes in *Patterson v. McLean Credit Union* (1989). Later in the chapter we will discuss his predictions in more detail, but for now, however, we reiterate the general logic regarding the importance of predicting coalitions.

First, demonstrating that justices systematically predict their colleagues' votes and the coalitions that ensue from these votes represents prima facie evidence that the coalition-formation process begins before the post–oral argument conference discussion among justices. More to the point, the assumption that the predictions are more accurate than chance predictions suggests that the seeds for winning coalitions are often sowed during oral argument—the fundamental theme of this book. Second, and perhaps more important, as a practical matter, successful predictions enable justices to build road maps of cases, providing them with knowledge about those issues on which their colleagues will base their decisions and what legal arguments may or may not be viable. By way of comparison, the Court often uses oral arguments "to get a better sense of the outer limits of an advocate's position" (Frederick 2003, 6), which is why justices ask hypothetical questions during these proceedings (Frederick 2003). The justices then use their ability to think forward as they determine how to set legal policy as close to their preferred position as possible (Murphy 1964; Epstein and Knight 1998).

When the Court hears oral argument in a case, the final coalition is usually several months (and sometimes more than a year) from coalescing. Despite this time lag, and with not one word of the majority draft written, it is possible to discern the justices' probable voting patterns based on conditions related to their ideological beliefs and behavior during these proceedings. We support this conjecture with evidence from Blackmun, who predicted coalitions in a significant number of cases in which he was involved. Our process involves several steps. First, we provide examples from several Supreme Court cases to demonstrate how he predicted votes and outcomes. Then we test whether his behavior was more systematic than anecdotal by examining two questions: (1) Under what conditions did Blackmun attempt to predict the vote of one of his colleagues, and (2) what factors explain whether Blackmun's vote predictions were accurate?

Coalition Predictions

In *Cruzan v. Missouri Dept. of Health* (1990), the Court was asked to determine whether the Due Process Clause of the Fourteenth Amendment permitted Nancy Cruzan's parents the right to refuse life-sustaining feeding and hydration tubes for their daughter. The case came to the Court after twenty-five-year-old Nancy Cruzan was involved in a 1983 car accident that left her in a persistent vegetative state. The case was controversial because it directly pitted two camps against each other—those who believe in the right to die versus those who support the right to live. The case hinged on whether the state of Missouri could require "clear and convincing" evidence that a person in a vegetative state wanted to be removed from life support. The Court ruled that this evidentiary burden was not met and therefore found constitutional the Missouri Supreme Court's decision to preserve Cruzan's life.

Based on what he heard his colleagues say during oral argument in *Cruzan,* Blackmun had no doubt about the outcome. Indeed, figure 25 shows his notes and (in the lower left corner) predictions in *Cruzan.*

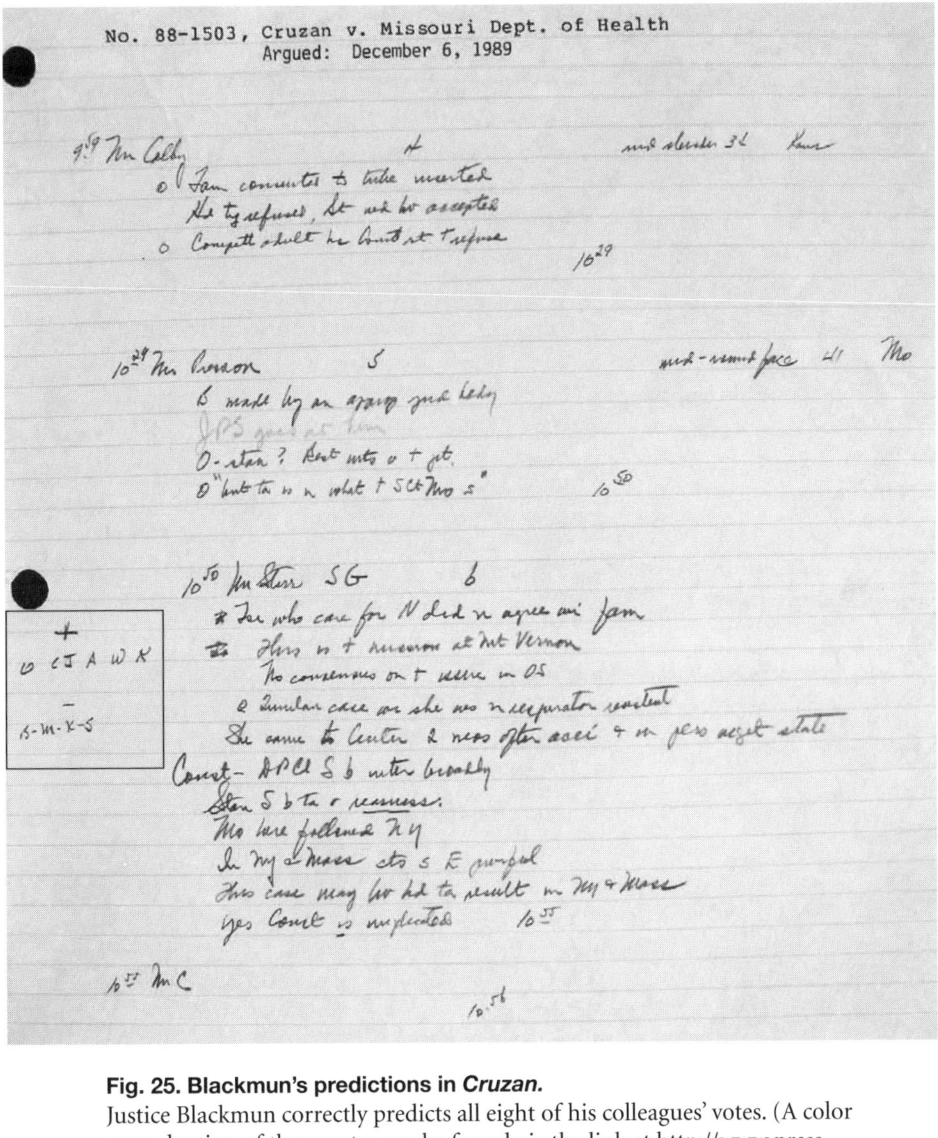

No. 88-1503, Cruzan v. Missouri Dept. of Health
Argued: December 6, 1989

Fig. 25. Blackmun's predictions in *Cruzan.*
Justice Blackmun correctly predicts all eight of his colleagues' votes. (A color reproduction of these notes can be found via the link at http://www.press.umich.edu/titleDetailDesc.do?id=4599894.)

Blackmun predicted "O CJ A W K" (Sandra Day O'Connor, William Rehnquist, Antonin Scalia, Byron R. White, and Anthony Kennedy) would vote to affirm, indicated by the plus sign.[1] Conversely, Blackmun predicted "B-M-X-S" (William J. Brennan, Thurgood Marshall, Blackmun himself, and John Paul Stevens) would vote to reverse, as indicated by the minus sign.

Blackmun was 100 percent correct: These are the coalitions that formed after conference and the opinion-writing process. What helped him accurately assess such a highly salient case? For us, the answer is obvious: His notes about his colleagues' questioning at oral arguments. For example, on the second line under "Respondent's Attorney," Blackmun writes in green pencil, "JPS goes at him," indicating that Stevens was giving the attorney for the state of Missouri a difficult time. This observation is supported by the oral argument transcript, which shows that Stevens spoke twenty-five times during the respondent's allotted time. In the following exchange, Scalia seems pleasant and helpful toward the attorney representing the state of Missouri, while Stevens is much more aggressive as he probes the limits of Missouri's argument:

JUSTICE SCALIA: The question whether they can be compelled to pay is quite separate, I assume, from the question of whether they have the right to demand that the—that the life of the individual not be continued.

MR. PRESSON: I, I would agree; that is a separate question.

JUSTICE STEVENS: Mr. Presson, you started your argument by saying that the state has the right to have a judicial officer make a decision of this kind. Under Missouri law, could the judge ever authorize the withdrawal of the life support procedures if there was no certain evidence with regard to the intent of the patient? Could there ever be circumstances that would justify that?

MR. PRESSON: I believe from my reading of the Missouri Supreme Court opinion, yes, that could happen.

JUSTICE STEVENS: What—what kind of circumstances would justify that?

MR. PRESSON: Well, I don't know that we can be global or totally exclusive about it. Some factors, I think, were mentioned by the Missouri Supreme Court. They did mention the possibility of pain, the heroic or extraordinary nature of the treatment. For instance, if a patient, such as Nancy in this case, were to develop cancer, whether they would approve chemotherapy or major surgery. I think it would present an entirely different case to them.

JUSTICE STEVENS: Well, why—why—why would that be different? Is that just because it's a different amount of dollars and cents involved? Here it costs about 10,000 a month, supposing it cost 100,000 a month with all—

MR. PRESSON: I don't think, based upon the Supreme Court's analysis, it's just a matter of dollars and cents.

JUSTICE STEVENS: So dollars would not be relevant, even?

MR. PRESSON: I—I—well, they certainly didn't indicate that it would be.

JUSTICE STEVENS: The one factor that would be relevant would be discomfort to the patient, pain?

MR. PRESSON: That's not the only—I think they—

JUSTICE STEVENS: Well, what else would be?

MR. PRESSON: They indicated whether it would be ordinary or extraordinary care. In this instance—

JUSTICE STEVENS: But what's—why—why is that significant, except in a dollars and cents way? What difference does is make if it's three nurses instead of one, or two tubes instead of one? Why does that matter?

MR. PRESSON: Well, it would be a more invasive type procedure. The Petitioners have—

JUSTICE STEVENS: But if there is no pain involved, so what? Why does that make a difference? I don't understand.[2]

Blackmun's oral argument notes also contain several references to O'Connor as well as several notes about the relevant legal arguments in the case.[3] That he took such notes is important because when *Cruzan* came to the Court, Blackmun had been on the bench for almost three decades. The fact that he was still actively taking notes suggests that Blackmun did not stop learning about cases or his colleagues while they sat together in open court. In sum, his notes suggest that during oral arguments, Blackmun was able to form a firm understanding of how his colleagues felt about how to decide *Cruzan.*

But this is not an isolated case: Several additional examples support this point. For example, in *Spallone v. United States* (1990), the Court dealt with a minor procedural question, though race was the key issue. The city of Yonkers, New York, planned to build subsidized housing projects in an area already predominantly populated by minority groups, and litigation ensued under Title VII of the Civil Rights Act. The lower court issued orders against the city and council members (including Henry Spallone) to desegregate the residential housing; after extensive delay, the council members were held in contempt by the judge and sanctioned. These sanctions were not minor. Each member remaining in contempt was fined one hundred dollars the first day, with the fine doubling for each consecutive day of noncompliance. Further, any member who failed to comply by August 10, 1998, would be committed to the custody of the U.S. Marshal. The Supreme Court examined whether a district court could impose such sanctions on specific council members.

Blackmun's oral arguments notes in *Spallone* provide an illuminating example of these proceedings' power to provide a road map for the Court's action. Figure 26 shows his notes on the case, with the predictions again in the lower left. Here, Blackmun correctly predicts seven of his colleagues' votes and makes clear how he personally will vote.

Two other features of Blackmun's notes are particularly informative. First, he is uncertain about how O'Connor will vote, as indicated by "O?"[4] O'Connor was the crucial fifth vote (as she was in many cases during her tenure on the bench) for whatever coalition she would join, and Blackmun simply could not get a handle on which way she would go based on what he saw during oral arguments. Second, and perhaps somewhat surprisingly, on the very bottom line, in green pencil, Blackmun notes "CJ will assign to himself." Rehnquist indeed wrote the majority opinion.[5] Thus, in *Spallone* at least, Blackmun gleaned more information from oral argument than simply the probable voting patterns.

In *Cruzan,* Blackmun's predictions were exactly correct.[6] In other cases (e.g., *Spallone*), however, he seemed less than sure about his colleagues. *Tower v. Glover* (1984) provides an example, as he wrote " –5-4, I would guess or +5-4."[7] Here, he predicted that he, Brennan, Marshall, and White would affirm, while Burger, Rehnquist, and O'Connor would reverse. He was unsure how Stevens and Powell would vote. In short, Blackmun did not attempt to predict the ultimate position of all of his colleagues in every case, and even when he did make such predictions, he expressed uncertainty from time to time about individual votes and about the ultimate outcome.

Even when Blackmun was uncertain, he occasionally ventured an educated guess. In *Barnes v. Glen Theatre Inc.* (1991), when deciding whether a state prohibition against complete nudity in a public place violated the First Amendment, Blackmun correctly predicted that there would be five votes to reverse and four to affirm. However, when he made his predictions, he placed question marks next to the names of four of the justices. This uncertainty was well founded, as he made two mistakes: He predicted that Scalia would be in the minority to affirm and White would be in the majority to reverse.[8]

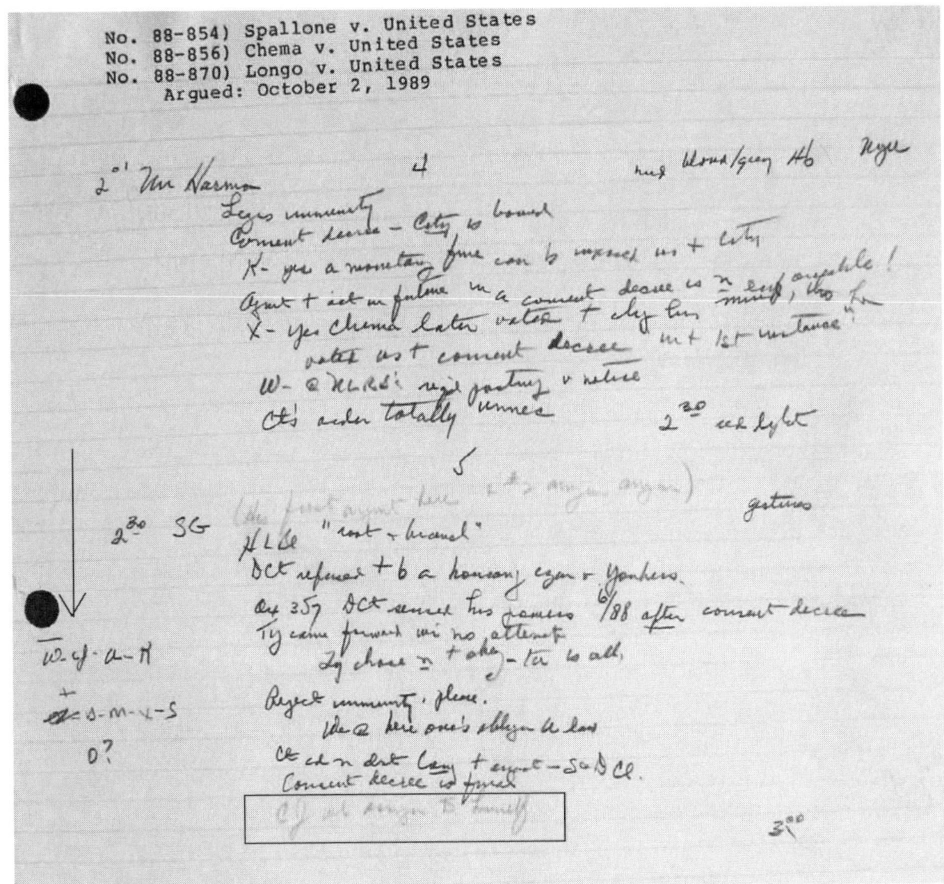

No. 88-854) Spallone v. United States
No. 88-856) Chema v. United States
No. 88-870) Longo v. United States
Argued: October 2, 1989

Fig. 26. Blackmun's predictions in *Spallone.* Blackmun correctly predicts seven of his colleague's votes plus himself but is uncertain about O'Connor. Additionally, Blackmun correctly predicts that Rehnquist will assign the case to himself. (A color reproduction of these notes can be found via the link at http://www.press.umich.edu/titleDetailDesc.do?id=4599894.)

In other cases, Blackmun seemed especially confident in the signals he heard at oral argument. During its 1991 term, when the Court sat for arguments in *Smith v. Barry* (1992), he wrote in his notes, "Justices telegraph their posit[ions]—CJ—A—K." Similarly, during oral argument in *Williams v. Zbaraz* and *Harris v. McRae,* the abortion cases decided during the 1979 term, Blackmun noted, "All Justices in their questions telegraph their attitudes. Result will be 6-3 or 5-4 to reverse." Here, too, Blackmun proved prophetic. By a 5-4 vote, the Court reversed the lower court and upheld the Hyde Amendment, which prohibited the use of Medicaid funds to pay for discretionary abortions.[9]

These examples indicate that during oral arguments, Blackmun sometimes attempted to predict case outcomes as well as how some or all of his colleagues would vote. Significant variation exists in the frequency with which he predicted his colleagues' votes, however. Across his career, Blackmun made predictions for about 8 percent of the total votes cast by participating justices, but he attempted to predict at least one of his colleagues' votes in 19 percent of those cases. But what systematic factors explain the variation in Blackmun's predictions? We now turn to answering this question.

Expectations and Hypotheses

Several general factors may correspond with Blackmun's prediction behavior. First, consistent with the general argument advanced in earlier chapters, we believe that he will make predictions to help him come to terms with the coalitions that might eventually form between him and his colleagues. In addition, we believe he uses these proceedings to build himself a map that enhances his ability to be forward-thinking as the Court moved toward the resolution of a case. Similarly, we posit that Blackmun's decision to make a prediction—and whether his prediction was accurate—is a function of the quality of information he possessed.

We turn first to two hypotheses that tap into the forward-looking component of Blackmun's behavior. The median justice, of course, plays a critical role in the Court's coalition-formation process. While the final legal policy set in an opinion may not fall at the median's ideal point (see, e.g., Bonneau et al. 2007; Carrubba et al. 2007), the median's influence over case outcomes and its ability to set boundaries on opinion content are difficult to deny (Maltzman, Spriggs, and Wahlbeck 2000). As a consequence of the centrality of the median and those close to that justice, we hypothesize:

> *Hypothesis 1:* Blackmun is more likely to predict (and to successfully predict) the votes of justices who are ideologically closer to the Court's median justice.[10]

While Blackmun tries to pinpoint potential swing justices, he is also likely to think about justices who are ideologically removed from his position. While such extremists are unlikely to be pivotal, an estimate of their vote can still provide useful information during the general coalition-formation process. That is, as Blackmun tries to determine what coalitions may form, he is likely to consider the boundaries set by justices who sit at the ideological poles. Once these outer boundaries have been identified, he can fill in the blanks about where others may ultimately come down in the case. This idea, too, is consistent with our argument from chapter 3 that significant value can be gained from knowing the preferences of those justices who are ideologically distant from the recording justice. Accordingly, we suggest:

> *Hypothesis 2:* Blackmun is more likely to predict (and successfully predict) the votes of justices who are ideologically distant from him.

Beyond strategic motivations, we contend that informational components also exercise a strong role in Blackmun's prediction behavior. In particular, we argue that he is more likely to predict his colleagues' positions and to have more success in so doing if they ask more questions and make more comments during these proceedings. The point is obvious: When a justice speaks more often, he or she is more likely to reveal information about his or her preferences regarding outcomes. Blackmun thus should be better equipped to predict how that justice will decide. This leads us to expect that:

> *Hypothesis 3:* Blackmun is both more likely to predict (and to be more successful at predicting) colleagues' votes in a case when he has taken more notes regarding their comments during oral argument.

While the most useful type of information will come from insights gleaned about specific colleagues through their statements during oral argument, other, more general information should aid Blackmun as well. Accordingly, we suggest:

> *Hypothesis 4:* Blackmun is both more likely to predict (and to be more successful at predicting) colleagues' votes in a case when he has taken more general (i.e., non-colleague-specific) notes during oral argument.

In addition to the information Blackmun specifically collects during a case, other, more general informational aspects of his relationship with colleagues and case characteristics should affect his prediction behavior.

Like all decision makers, justices learn from prior interaction with colleagues. The literature in judicial politics also indicates the presence of a "freshman effect" on the Supreme Court, whereby it takes new justices a few years to adjust to being on the nation's highest bench (Hagle 1993b). Blackmun indeed suggested that this freshman effect made it more difficult to determine how new justices would act. Expounding on the different institutional powers possessed by Supreme Court justices and lower-court judges, he stated, "[T]he unique opportunity to develop one's constitutional philosophy made predictions about how a new justice would vote problematic" (Strum 2000, 295). Thus, the longer justices serve together on the Court, the better able they should be to anticipate their colleagues' preferences and likely choices in a case. We therefore predict that:

> *Hypothesis 5:* The longer Blackmun has served on the Court with other justices, the more likely he is to predict (and to successfully predict) their vote.

It is also likely that variation in Blackmun's level of expertise in different issue areas contributed to his ability to predict accurately his colleagues' votes. Several lines of reasoning lead us to this conjecture. First, because opinion authors decide whether to accommodate their colleagues' preferences (Maltzman, Spriggs, and Wahlbeck 2000), the more Blackmun was assigned to write on an issue, the more correspondence he had with his colleagues' about their preferences on that issue. This correspondence should inform Blackmun about his colleagues' preferences in future cases and allow him to make more accurate predictions on those issues. Second, Maltzman and Wahlbeck (2004) find that the chief justice is more likely to assign opinions to justices who have established their expertise in an area of the law, at least in part because those justices have shown an interest in that area. As Blackmun develops expertise, he likely also develops an interest in the area or at least an increased expectation that he will receive the opinion assignment. Thus, he should be more inclined to gather information about his colleagues' preferences, leading to more accurate predictions. Accordingly, we expect:

> *Hypothesis 6:* Blackmun is more likely to predict (and to successfully predict) the votes of justices in cases involving issues where he has more expertise than when he is less familiar with a topic.

Finally, a plethora of evidence indicates that in complex cases, justices are less sure of their position on the merits (e.g., Maltzman, Spriggs, and Wahlbeck 2000; Collins 2008b). Thus, Blackmun should be less likely to make predictions about his colleagues in complicated cases.[11] And when he has ventured a guess about a vote in these cases, his predictions should be less accurate. Thus, we expect:

Hypothesis 7: Blackmun is less likely to predict (and to successfully predict) his colleagues' votes in legally complex cases.

Data and Methods

To test our hypotheses, we return to Blackmun's oral argument notes and examine each page to determine whether he attempted to predict a colleague's vote and, if so, how he thought each colleague would vote. As already noted, Blackmun predicted an overall total of 8 percent of his colleagues' votes but made at least one vote prediction in 19 percent of the cases heard during his career. We merged these data with data obtained from the Supreme Court Judicial Database on each justice's reported (i.e., final) merits vote, which allows us to assess the accuracy of Blackmun's predictions.

Blackmun's speculations were accurate in just over 75 percent of the roughly 1,800 predictions he made. Figure 27 illustrates the term-by-term success rate for his predictions. Specifically, the figure shows the number of predictions Blackmun made each term, the proportion correct and incorrect, and the overall percentage correct. Blackmun was slow to make predictions during his first decade on the bench but then became a fairly regular forecaster. His accuracy rate, however, remained relatively constant, usually in the mid-70s.

For our dependent variable, three possible outcomes exist: (1) Blackmun does not attempt to predict his colleague's vote, (2) Blackmun unsuccessfully predicts his colleague's vote, and (3) Blackmun successfully predicts his colleague's vote. We expect a relationship to exist between Blackmun's decision to make a prediction and the eventual accuracy of that prediction. That is, we expect that Blackmun is systematically less likely to attempt a prediction if he thought he could not do so accurately. Accordingly, the probability that his prediction is accurate is almost certainly correlated with his initial decision to attempt a prediction. To account for this relationship (and for other methodological reasons de-

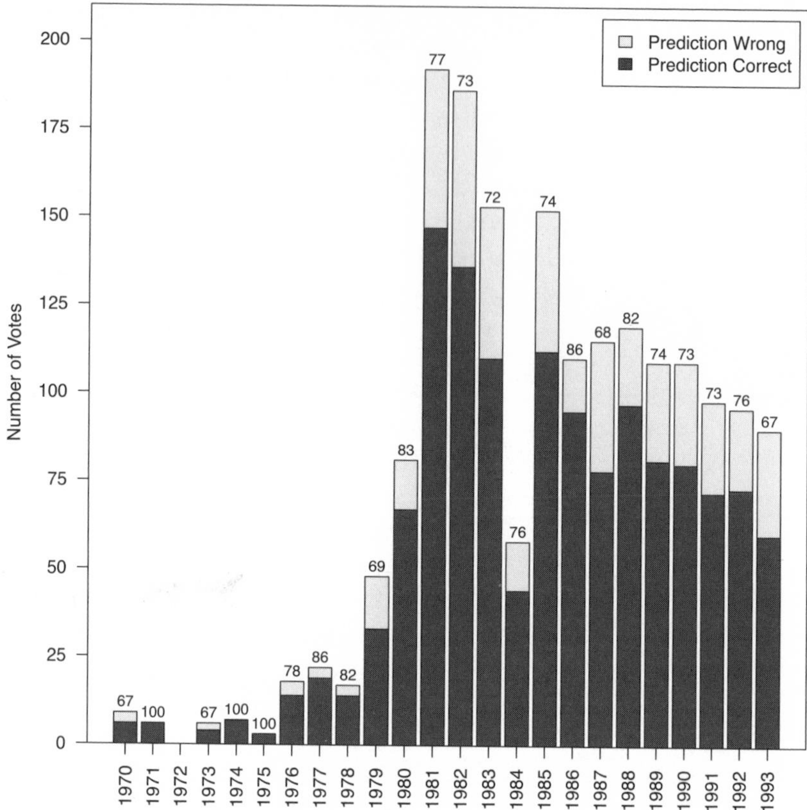

Fig. 27. Justice Blackmun's predictions by term. The size of the bars represents the number of votes for which Blackmun attempted a prediction for each term. The dark shadings represent correct predictions and the light shadings represent wrong predictions. The numbers above the bars are the percentage of correct predictions within each term.

scribed in the appendix to the chapter) we estimate a Sartori (2003) selection model.[12]

All seven of our independent variables have appeared in previous chapters and, with one exception, are measured in an identical manner. We now operationalize our *Issue Expertise* variable as the (rolling) percentage of opinions in an issue area where Blackmun has written an opinion. Our previous usage of this variable subtracted a colleague's expertise score from Blackmun's because a relative measure was more appropriate. In this context, we focus on the raw amount of information Blackmun possesses.[13]

Results

Table 4 reports parameter estimates for our model. The top half of the table corresponds to the selection equation of whether Blackmun attempted to predict each of his colleague's votes. The bottom half presents estimates for the outcome equation that examines whether, given that Blackmun attempted a prediction, his speculation was correct.

The results reveal that several of our explanatory variables are statistically significant and signed in the expected direction. However, because of the nonlinearity of the model, the parameter estimates provide only a superficial snapshot of how the independent variables affect the dependent variable. We therefore turn to predicted probabilities to explicate the substantive nature of our results. We begin with our *Speaker's Distance from Median* variable (figure 28). We theorized that as a consequence of the fundamental spatial importance of the median justice, Blackmun would have more to gain strategically by attempting to predict how the median—or those justices who were close to the median—would vote.

TABLE 4. Justice Blackmun's Propensity to Predict His Colleague's Votes and to Predict Them Accurately

	Coefficient	Robust S.E.
Did Blackmun Attempt to Predict Vote?		
Speaker's Ideological Distance from Median	–0.129*	0.010
Ideological Distance	0.173*	0.012
Number of Speaker References	0.278*	0.024
Overall Amount of Oral Argument Notes	0.001	0.002
Length of Joint Service	0.044*	0.002
Issue Area Expertise	0.018*	0.001
Case Complexity	0.015*	0.003
Constant	–2.500*	0.048
Was Blackmun's Prediction Correct?		
Speaker's Ideological Distance from Median	–0.102*	0.011
Ideological Distance	0.154*	0.013
Number of Speaker References	0.237*	0.027
Overall Amount of Oral Argument Notes	0.001	0.002
Length of Joint Service	0.039*	0.002
Issue Area Expertise	0.016*	0.002
Case Complexity	0.017*	0.003
Constant	–2.556*	0.057
Observations	22,374	
Log likelihood	–6,755.585	

Note: The model is a Sartori selection model (see appendix for more details).
*denotes $p < 0.05$ (two-tailed test).

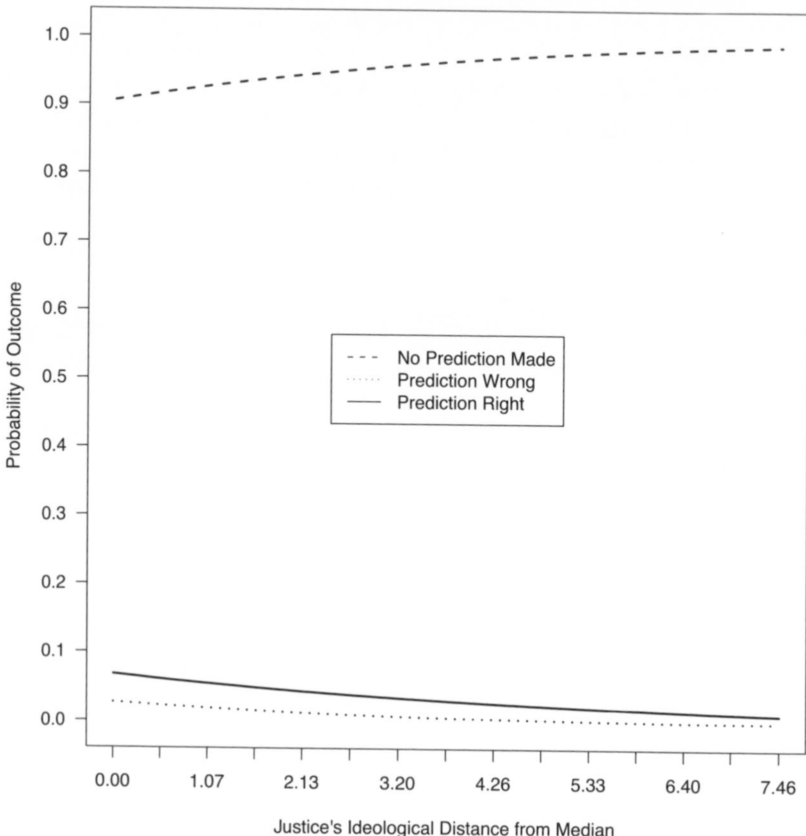

Fig. 28. Effect of distance from median on prediction behavior. Probability outcome space of Blackmun's efforts at predicting a colleague's vote, conditional on the ideological distance between the Court median and Blackmun's specific colleague. All other variables were held at their modal or mean values, as appropriate. Point estimates obtained through stochastic simulations similar to Clarify.

Our results support this hypothesis. When Blackmun's colleague is the median justice (i.e., has a distance value of zero), we estimate a probability of 0.10 that Blackmun attempts to predict that justice's vote. If he has attempted to predict the median justice's vote, we predict that he does so accurately about 70 percent of the time. By contrast, when the justice is maximally distant from the median, we estimate just over a 1 percent chance that Blackmun attempts to make a prediction.

We note two points about this finding. First, given that Blackmun seeks information from those who are ideologically distant, it is counterintuitive that he would be less likely to make a prediction as the distance between the justice and the median increases. Second, and perhaps more noteworthy, the distance from the median does not have an overwhelming effect on Blackmun's probability of venturing a guess. In other words, the *Speaker's Distance from Median* variable has a relatively small overall effect on Blackmun's prediction behavior. Indeed, while the ideological distance displayed on the x-axis is rather large, spanning from 0 (the median) to 7.46 units (the most distant justice in the data set), the change in probability is relatively small (0.09) and may appear marginal. These points suggest that Blackmun likely finds other criteria, such as the ideological distance between himself and his colleagues, more helpful in making predictions.

Our result for *Ideological Distance* (figure 29) corroborates this strategic intuition. In particular, our results suggest that the greater the distance between Blackmun and a colleague, the more likely he is both to attempt a prediction and to make an accurate prediction. This finding supports our initial hypothesis that Blackmun generated these predictions not out of boredom but rather to further clarify his view of the strategic terrain. Just as we observe in the previous chapter, by focusing on distant colleagues, Blackmun was likely able to identify the salient cleavages in a case and use those predictions to further clarify and refine his views.

Beyond the strategic dimension of Blackmun's prediction behavior, we also find evidence for the role played by factors related to the quality of information he possessed, as figure 30 illustrates. On the x-axis, we show the number of colleague-specific references made by Blackmun during oral argument. On the y-axis, we provide the predicted probability of different outcomes for our dependent variable.

When Blackmun notes no additional information about his colleague during oral argument, we estimate a 0.93 probability that he will opt to make no prediction of that colleague's vote. By contrast, when Blackmun has a much larger body of information—in the form of four colleague-specific references—we find the probability that he will not make a prediction plummets almost 30 percent to 0.65. Moreover, as the figure demonstrates, when Blackmun has a large amount of information from which to draw, his likelihood of making an accurate prediction increases. Blackmun is nearly two and half times more likely to make an accurate prediction than an incorrect one when he has four colleague references before him.

While we find a strong relationship between colleague-specific infor-

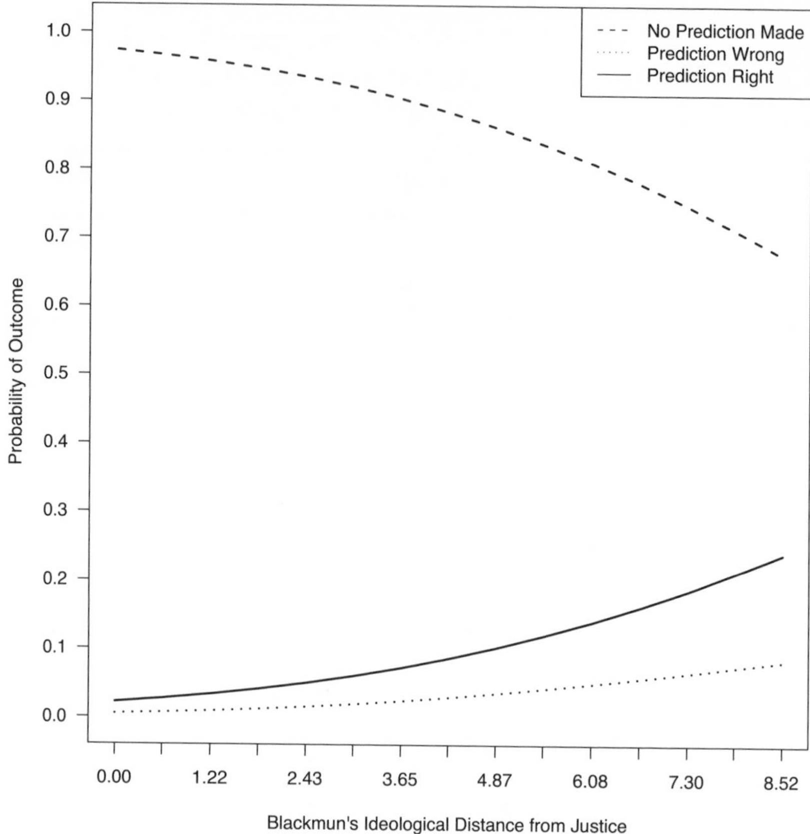

Fig. 29. Effect of ideological distance on prediction behavior. Probability outcome space of Blackmun's efforts at predicting a colleague's vote, conditional on the ideological distance between Blackmun and his colleague. All other variables were held at their modal or mean values, as appropriate. Point estimates obtained through stochastic simulations similar to Clarify.

mation and Blackmun's predictive behavior, the results in table 4 fail to find a similar relationship for the more general quantity of the overall number of notes taken by Blackmun. This finding suggests that more information is not necessarily better because the type or source of information is crucial. This result is noteworthy because of the informational role that oral arguments play. These findings suggest that justices do not use these proceedings to gather just any sort of information but rather seek specific types of information because of their utility in generating a road

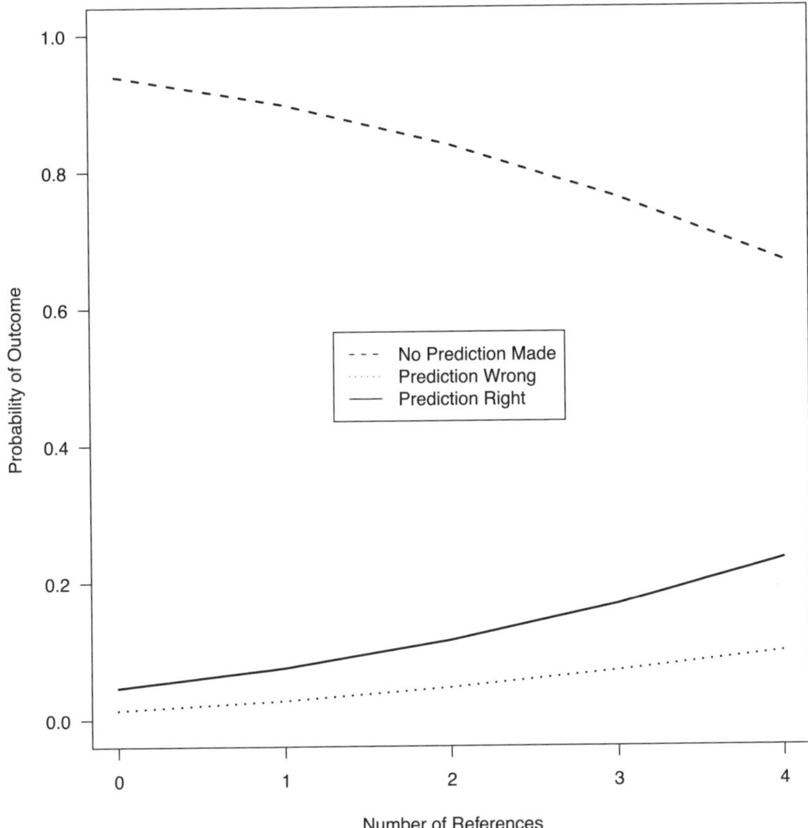

Fig. 30. Effect of colleague references on prediction behavior. Probability outcome space of Blackmun's efforts at predicting a colleague's vote, conditional on the number of colleague-specific references Blackmun took during oral arguments. All other variables were held at their modal or mean values, as appropriate. Point estimates obtained through stochastic simulations similar to Clarify.

map of the case. On the other hand, when the information comes directly from a colleague, more is better because it enables Blackmun to learn something about how that colleague might vote.

Our data do suggest as well the presence of a learning effect for Blackmun. As figure 31 shows, the longer Blackmun serves alongside a colleague, the more likely he is to try to predict that colleague's vote and the more likely he is to be accurate in his projection. During the freshman years of a justice's tenure on the Court, Blackmun was exceptionally un-

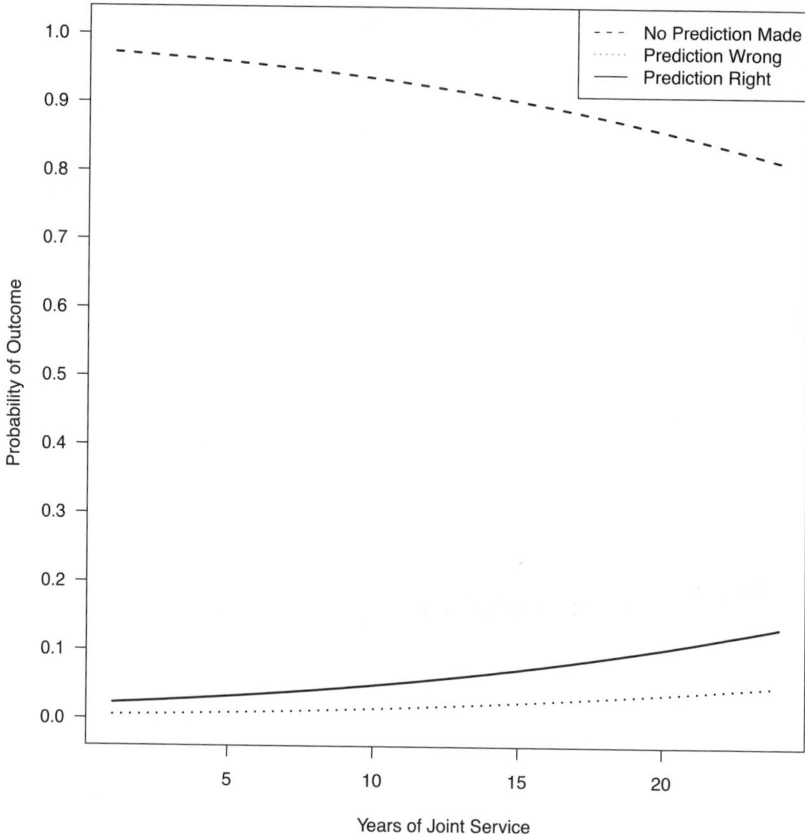

Fig. 31. Effect of joint service on prediction behavior. Probability outcome space of Blackmun's efforts at predicting a colleague's vote, conditional on the number of years of joint service between Blackmun and his colleague. All other variables were held at their modal or mean values, as appropriate. Point estimates obtained through stochastic simulations similar to Clarify.

likely to attempt to predict how that justice would vote. Indeed, when a justice had served only a single term alongside Blackmun, we estimate a 0.97 probability that Blackmun fails to attempt to predict that colleague's vote. By contrast, when Blackmun had served alongside his colleague for the sample maximum of 23 years, we observe almost a 20 percent reduction in the probability that Blackmun makes no prediction. And as the upward slope on the solid black line demonstrates, Blackmun's predictions become increasingly accurate as he gains information about his colleague's preferences.

Finally, figures 32 and 33 illustrate the effect of Blackmun's issue ex-

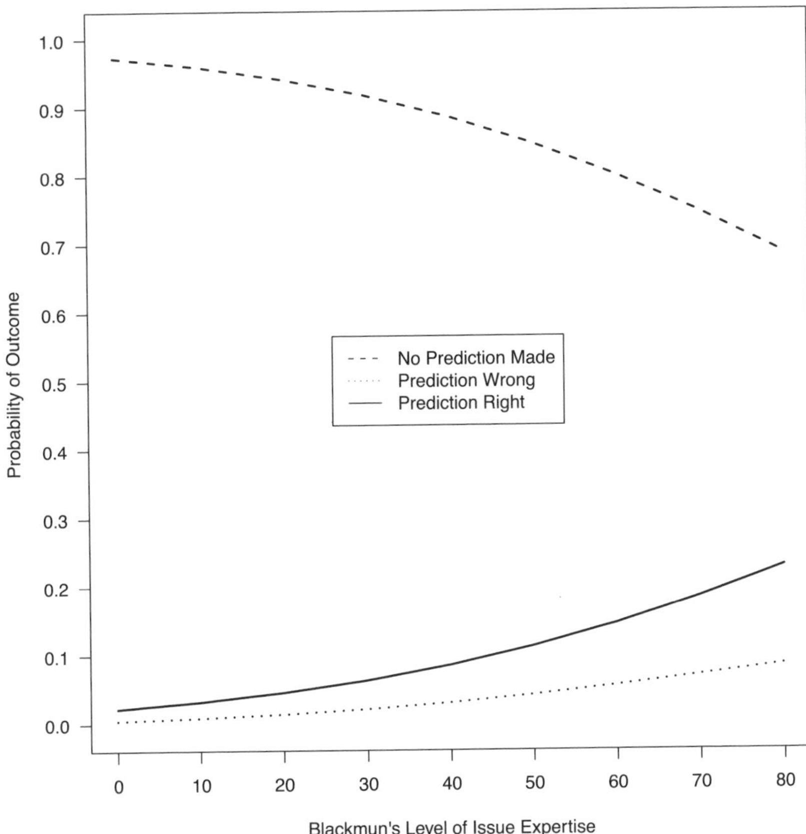

Fig. 32. Effect of expertise on prediction behavior. Probability outcome space of Blackmun's efforts at predicting a colleague's vote, conditional on Blackmun's relative issue expertise. Small values correspond to Blackmun having less expertise, and large values denote areas where Blackmun is more of an expert. All other variables were held at their modal or mean values, as appropriate. Point estimates obtained through stochastic simulations similar to Clarify.

pertise and the complexity of a case, respectively, on his prediction behavior. The x-axis in figure 32 denotes Blackmun's level of expertise, with small values denoting a relative unfamiliarity with an issue and large values indicating that he frequently wrote opinions in such cases. Consistent with our expectations, we find that Blackmun was both more likely to attempt a prediction and more likely to make a successful one when he was an issue expert. Specifically, when Blackmun is a complete novice, having written essentially zero opinions in an issue area, the probability that he

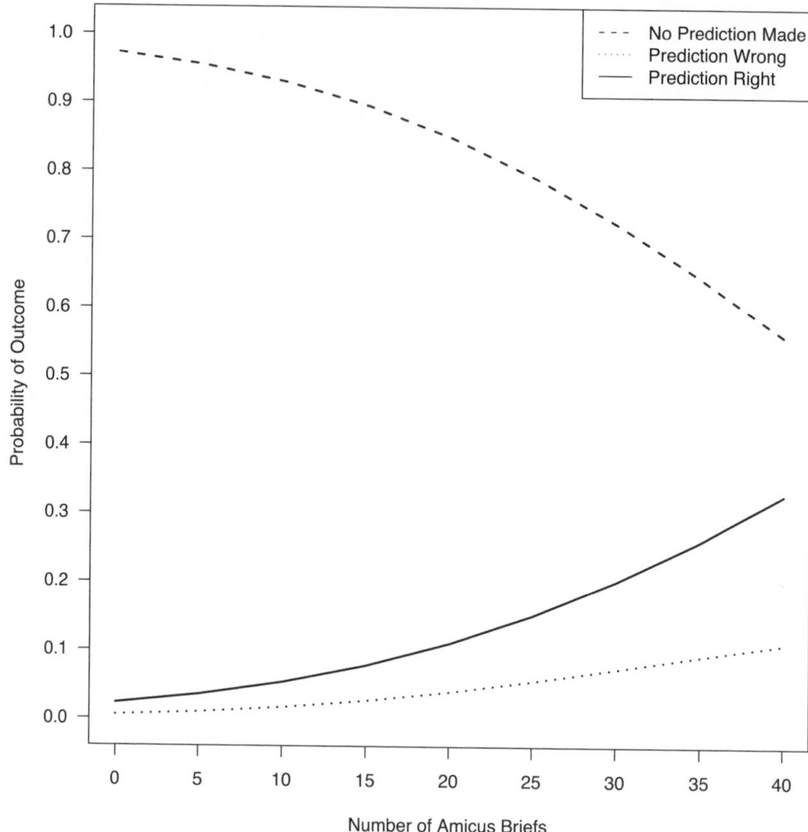

Fig. 33. Effect of case complexity on prediction behavior. Probability outcome space of Blackmun's efforts at predicting a colleague's vote, conditional on the level of case complexity (i.e., number of amicus briefs). All other variables were held at their modal or mean values, as appropriate. Point estimates obtained through stochastic simulations similar to Clarify.

will not make a prediction is approximately 0.97. However, after Blackmun writes many opinions in an issue area and develops a high level of expertise, we observe close to a 30 percent reduction in the probability that he makes no prediction. We also observe that expertise contributes greatly to his prediction success. For example, when Blackmun is a novice, the number of correct and incorrect predictions are virtually the same. However, after becoming an expert in an area of the law (and presumably his colleagues' preferences in that area), he is twice as likely to make a correct prediction as an incorrect prediction.

Contrary to our final hypothesis, we find both that Blackmun was more likely to make predictions in relatively complex cases and that those predictions were more likely to be accurate. While we hesitate to engage in too much post hoc speculation about why the data reveal this particular relationship, one partial explanation is that in preparing for the bargaining and opinion-writing stage in a complex case, the need for a prediction is higher than it is in simpler cases. Accordingly, Blackmun may have been more likely to make a prediction because doing so would help him clarify his thoughts and assess the likely sequence of events to come.

In other words, perhaps complex cases are precisely where more information is needed because of the presence of uncertainty in the outcome. With heightened uncertainty as a result of the added complexity of a case with multiple dimensions, the opportunity to gain a strategic victory substantially increases. Conversely, in a simple and straightforward case, more information will yield very little dividend because Blackmun and his colleagues likely already know on what grounds the case will be decided. If so, Blackmun may have seen little benefit in making predictions. This result would suggest that the payoff for gathering information about his colleagues during complex cases is substantially higher. Furthermore, while it seems mysterious that Blackmun's accuracy increased along with the complexity of the case, an increasing number of amicus briefs also represents an increase in information coming to the Court, and this information may help the justices better grasp the legal issues at stake. And at some point when a substantial number of amicus briefs have been submitted, some overlap among the perspectives of the amicus briefs will undoubtedly occur, causing the complexity of a case to reach a plateau. Thus, as more amicus briefs are pouring into the Court, their cumulative informational value helps justices overcome any initial uncertainty generated by the increased complexity.

Conclusion

Blackmun would take notes regarding his colleagues' questions and at times try to predict their ultimate votes on the merits. We contend that Blackmun recorded this information to assist him in assessing the positions of his colleagues and the issues in a case. Specifically, we argue that if the information he gleaned from oral arguments was valuable, we should find a strong and positive correlation between the frequency with which he records notes for a particular justice's questions at oral arguments and his attempts to predict that colleague's vote. The data analysis provides convincing support for this relationship and thus provides additional and robust evidence for the informational value of oral arguments in Supreme Court decision making.

Oral arguments are important for helping the justices better understand the case and the likely coalitions that will form. Indeed, former chief justice Charles Evans Hughes (1928, 61, 63) said as much when he explained that oral arguments help justices quickly grasp the case and "separate the wheat from the chaff." He went on to explain that his final impressions at oral argument often accorded with his final vote in most cases. For Blackmun, oral arguments appear to clarify not only the issue and outcome but also his views of how his colleagues would ultimately decide some of our nation's most difficult legal questions.

APPENDIX

Model Selection

The canonical approach to modeling a selection process is to estimate a Heckman-style selection model. Because both of our dependent variables (i.e., prediction attempted, prediction successful) are dichotomous, a Heckman probit model might seem appropriate. As an empirical matter, however, the use of the Heckman probit model is frequently problematic. Its estimation depends on the existence of at least one exclusionary variable. This is a variable that is related to the selection equation (i.e., prediction attempted) but is entirely unrelated to the outcome equation (i.e., prediction successful). The exclusionary variable (or variables) allows the model to be statistically identified and yield a set of meaningful parameter estimates.

Some research topics provide natural exclusionary variables. For example, Solowiej and Brunell (2003) study whether widows of members of the House of Representatives decide to succeed their husbands. The selection stage is whether a member dies, which is modeled as a function of his age. As there is no theoretical reason to believe that the age of a deceased husband influences the widow's decision to assume his seat, the authors have included a valid exclusionary restriction (see also Nicholson and Collins 2008).

In the context of our analysis, however, no such variable appears to exist. Each of the seven variables in the selection equation has an entirely plausible relationship with our outcome variable. Hence, any variable that we arbitrarily decide to omit from the outcome equation is all but guaranteed to induce omitted variable bias in that equation.

Moreover, recent scholarship on Heckman-style selection models suggests that poorly identified models (i.e., those without proper exclusionary restrictions) frequently yield erroneous inferences and biased parameter estimates (Brandt and Schneider 2007; Freedman and Sekhon 2010). As a result, we could not follow the tack of other studies and estimate a Heckman-style model.

Of course, we are not the first to encounter the dilemma of having identical variables for the selection and outcome equations. To address this concern, Sartori (2003) proposes an estimator to be deployed when faced with such a problem. Whereas the traditional Heckman model is identified through the exclusionary variable, Sartori's estimator is identified by assuming that the error terms across both equations are equal. Doing so allows the user to include identical variables in the selection and outcome equations.

Model Specification

In specifying the model predictors, we also considered explicitly modeling Blackmun's uncertainty as an independent variable. Specifically, we considered including a variable that accounts for the instances when Blackmun placed a question mark by the initials of the justice whose vote he was trying to predict. However, doing so would present two problems. First, the Sartori selection model requires that both sets of predictors be identical, and including uncertainty in the second equation would violate that principle. Thus, if we explicitly modeled uncertainty as an independent variable, we could include it only in a single equation model, eschewing the Sartori model altogether. That approach would leave us with the vexing problem of failing to account for the connection between making a prediction and the accuracy of that prediction. Second, modeling uncertainty as an independent variable would still not solve the identification problem for a Heckman selection model. Thus, we chose to account for uncertainty with the modeling process and not as an independent variable, a tack we feel better represents the underlying issue by using a Sartori selection model to account for the fact that making a prediction was related to the success of that prediction.

Unsurprisingly, however, Blackmun's prediction success rate decreases when he expresses uncertainty about his guess. Indeed, 64.6 percent of his predictions are accurate when he follows the prediction with a question mark. When the marker of uncertainty is not present, however, 76 percent of Blackmun's predictions are accurate ($p = 0.002$).

Blackmun's Individual-Level Prediction Rates

Figure 34 illustrates Blackmun's accuracy at predicting the votes of individual justices.

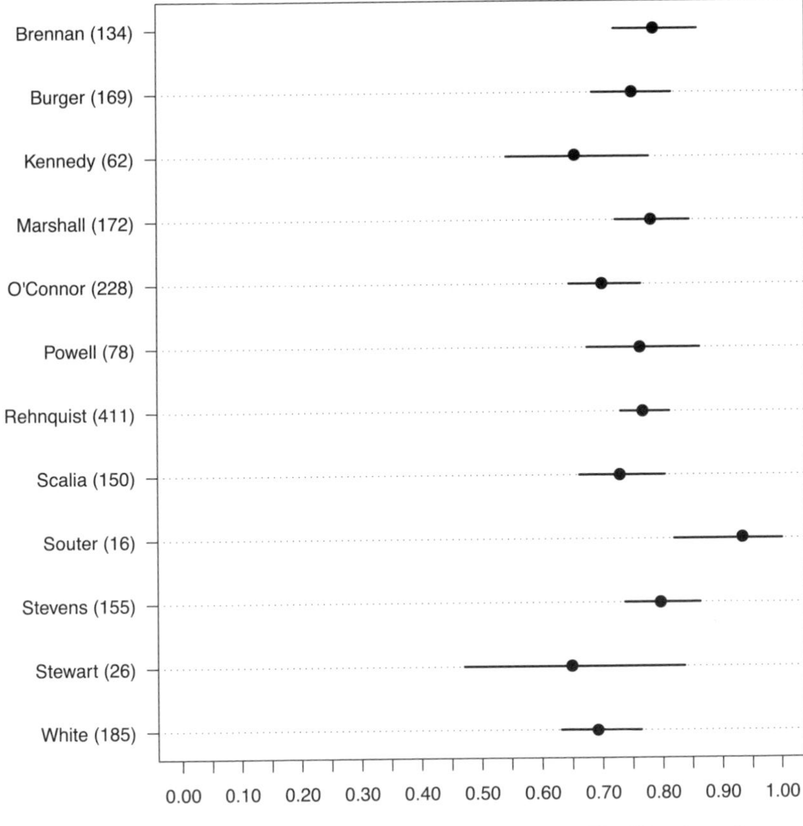

Fig. 34. Justice Blackmun's individual justice predictions. Dot plot of Justice Blackmun's success at predicting his colleagues' final merits votes. Numbers in parentheses denote the number of cases where Blackmun made a prediction. The thick horizontal whiskers denote 95% confidence intervals around the point estimates (two-tailed). We exclude several justices for whom the number of vote predictions was below 15. These include Black (2 for 2), Douglas (6 for 7), Ginsburg (3 for 3), Harlan (1 for 1), and Thomas (4 for 5). Blackmun's success rate was relatively accurate and constant across justices, with the exception of Souter, however, with whom he was much more accurate.

5 | Conclusion

The Importance of Oral Arguments as a Conversation

In chapter 1, we began with two simple arguments about how coalitions form during a decision-making process. First, the commencement of any coalition-formation process is a vital component in understanding what coalitions will form when decisions are finally made. Second, face-to-face communication among those involved in group decision making may be the best way for coalitions to form. The evidence we have brought to bear in the remainder of the book supports these two contentions.

More specifically, our central theme is that oral arguments begin the coalition-formation process for Supreme Court justices and that these face-to-face discussions point clearly to how cases will be decided. Evidence of these conversations can be seen when justices interrupt their colleagues in open court, when they take notes while listening and learning about their colleagues' views on a case, and when they use what they learn during these conversations to predict the final coalition and case outcomes. These conversations ultimately indicate that oral arguments play an integral role in how the Court decides cases.

This theme is important because the Supreme Court crafts, shapes, and molds law on the most pressing legal matters facing the nation—abortion, the death penalty, affirmative action. These issues are not typically new to the public sphere in any real sense; they have often been discussed in the larger policy arena by the president, members of Congress, and lower courts. In fact, by the time a case reaches the Supreme Court, most citizens are likely to have formed at least an initial opinion on the issue, though these opinions may still be malleable. Given that other actors have usually discussed, debated, and rhetoricized each topic at great length, it may be surprising that the justices' conversations at oral argument can play such an important role in the outcome of a case. That these proceedings have any impact at all on the Court's legal policy outcomes lies in direct contrast to the conventional wisdom of only a decade ago, when oral advocacy was often seen as a mere formality, with the case's outcome predetermined by the law or by the personal attitudes and views of the justices (Segal and Spaeth 2002).

As examples from the first four chapters of this book illustrate, however, justices often literally talk among themselves and ignore what attorneys are saying. To us, these examples demonstrate vividly how justices interrupt one another, gauge their colleagues' views, and estimate the likely final coalition based on the conversation at oral argument. In this chapter, we summarize and consider our key findings before discussing their broad implications for the Supreme Court and our political institutions in general and for the formation of coalitions. We close the chapter with some discussion of the direction of future research on these grand conversations and some thoughts on the role of oral arguments in the coalition-formation process.

What We Found: A Final Evaluation

In each chapter, we examined a specific aspect of oral argument and showed how it contributed to the coalition-formation process. Each of these components is unique and, with only limited exceptions, has not previously been examined. We also connected these unique behaviors to a larger set of general principles about how individuals behave on the Supreme Court and in small groups generally. Moreover, we documented how coalitions originate, moving from nine individual views to a court with connections among justices.

In chapter 2 we showed that justices speaking over each other (our definition of an interruption) is a central part of oral arguments. While most scholars of the Court are well aware that justices interrupt attorneys, very little systematic evidence exists regarding such behavior. This gap is striking given that we found that interruptions occur an average of approximately eight times per case. Moreover, we showed that these interruptions follow a logical pattern, with justices more likely to interrupt ideologically distant colleagues. This finding holds even after accounting for other plausible explanations, the most interesting of which is that justices punish other justices who violate the norm of collegiality. That is, justices who were the victim of an interruption by a particular colleague are more likely to punish the perpetrator later in the proceedings. This finding supports the contention that justices view oral arguments as something of a competitive game and that interruptions may signal to other justices that the interrupter does not like a particular line of questioning or hopes to hinder the other justices' learning efforts.

The results in chapter 3 also support our theoretical argument that justices learn about cases during oral arguments. As circuit court judge Frank M. Coffin put it, "How often I have begun argument with a clear idea of the strength or weakness of the decision being appealed, only to realize from a colleague's questioning that there was much, much more to the case than met my eye" (qtd. in Garner 2009, 3). Specifically, we found that the justices are likely to listen to their colleagues on the bench and that this phenomenon is strongly related to the ideological distance between the justices. We found that justices differ in to whom they listen. Lewis F. Powell appears to note comments from close ideological allies while Harry A. Blackmun appears to note comments from those ideologically more distant. In addition, we found that Blackmun is more likely than Powell to refer to a colleague's utterance at oral argument when that colleague is close to the median. Combined, these results suggest that although Powell and Blackmun focus on different types of colleagues, both men use oral arguments to help them figure out whom they will need to build a coalition.

Once we established the systematic factors that explain to whom justices listen, we then set out to explain how they use that information when forming coalitions. Specifically, we sought to determine whether note taking bears any relationship to how justices respond to draft majority opinions circulated by either Blackmun or Powell. We found that the two justices received similar patterns of responses from their colleagues based on how much they took notes about what their colleagues said during oral arguments. The natural leap we draw from this finding is that when justices learn about their colleagues' focus during oral arguments, they use this information to craft opinions these colleagues are more likely to join. This is akin to the preemptive accommodation hypothesis forwarded by Maltzman, Spriggs, and Wahlbeck (2000).

The results from chapter 4 should put to rest any doubt that the coalition-formation process begins during oral arguments. Indeed, Blackmun's oral argument notes clearly show that he was predicting likely final coalitions as he sat in open court. Specifically, we found that Blackmun predicted approximately 8 percent of his colleagues' votes and made at least one vote prediction in 19 percent of the cases he heard. In addition, we also found that the more Blackmun notes comments from a specific colleague, the more likely he is to predict that colleague's vote. Blackmun is no amateur sidewalk fortune-teller. When he ventures a prediction, he is correct about 76 percent of the time, a figure that increases to 80 percent when he notes two or more references. We believe that this finding offers solid evidence that learning at oral arguments pays off in terms of helping justices build a road map of the likely path a case will take.

In sum, the analysis we present throughout the book provides a great deal of information about how Supreme Court oral arguments contribute to the coalition-formation process. Perhaps more important, the analysis also teaches us that scholars must look to the oral arguments rather than to a later aspect of the decision-making process as they analyze the factors that lead justices to join (or refuse to join) particular coalitions.

The Implications of Oral Arguments as a Conversation between Justices

When oral arguments are viewed as a conversation among justices and not as a simple formality that allows justices to gather an occasional odd detail about a case, they quickly become an integral part of the process of how cases are decided by the U.S. Supreme Court. Furthermore, when oral arguments are established as the beginning of the coalition-formation process, their importance ascends even farther. What does this mean for the Supreme Court more generally?

In their seminal work on the opinion-writing process, Maltzman, Spriggs, and Wahlbeck (2000) systematically demonstrate that the justices' decisions are not driven solely by their personal policy preferences. At the key stages of crafting a majority opinion, decisions are based on the behavior, signals, and preferences of the other justices. Yet Maltzman, Spriggs, and Wahlbeck stop short of explaining the content of Court opinions. We pick up where they ended by showing how conversations during oral arguments represent the seeds of the final opinions. This is evidenced by the transcripts and notes we use to analyze Blackmun and Powell's behavior. In other words, the crafting of the majority opinion has its roots as far back in the process as the oral arguments. While research has shown that litigants' legal briefs have some correspondence with the content of the majority opinion (Corley 2008; Wedeking 2010), we show that because oral arguments represent the first time all the justices gather in one place to discuss the merits of the case, these proceedings represent the first stage of the coalescing of outcomes. It is where the rubber meets the road, so to speak—where the information contained in the briefs and the justices' questions and concerns converge to begin to create a final opinion. Our analysis implies that oral arguments provide the foundation for the resolution of most cases.

These findings also speak to a major topic of discussion among appellate-level attorneys and appellate judges alike—whether oral arguments should be eliminated altogether. While calls for this action are still in the minority, the Supreme Court has, over time, devoted substantially less time to these proceedings. Today, the typical case allows thirty minutes for each side, but it is not uncommon for some of that time to be split with another party or with the solicitor general. Moreover, because of the Court's shrinking plenary docket, oral arguments occur in fewer and fewer cases each term. At some point, we expect that these downward trends will either level off or disappear altogether. However, our findings allow us to speculate about what might happen should the Court decide to altogether eliminate oral arguments from its decision-making process.

We believe that the elimination of oral arguments would be a strong blow to the Court's process of crafting law. It would remove one of the important venues in which justices converse with each other about the case, determine their concerns about particular issues, and begin learning how eventual coalitions might form. Without oral arguments, we would expect that the opinion-writing process would be less efficient and more time-consuming as would-be opinion authors (at least initially) would have substantially less information about their colleagues' positions.

Such action would also eliminate the only public portion of the Court's decision-making process and thus would remove the only bit of transparency in the nation's court of last resort. While our system of separate powers specifically insulates the judiciary, the Court is still responsible for making decisions consistent with the Constitution. If oral arguments are eliminated, then the attorneys will less effectively represent their client's constitutional interests and respond to the justices' comments and queries about a case. Moreover, with one fewer stage in the decision-making process, we may see fewer opinions signed by at least five justices. While these contentions are speculative, they are a possibility if the justices' most important group communication forum is removed. Fewer majority opinions (and more plurality opinions) would mean that the Supreme Court would no longer satisfy one of its main goals—to clarify law for lower courts, the legal community, and the public. Viewed in this light, oral arguments then become a key cog in the machine of democratic governance even though the Court is the one nondemocratic institution in our federal system.

Finally, we noted in chapter 1 that very little of the literature on coalition formation documents how individuals gather information and signal one another as they coordinate their preferences into a group decision. This lacuna exists not only in coalition work on the courts but also in work on political coalitions more generally. Our results imply that a public forum where key decision makers gather information and signal one another serves a vital function. Moreover, these findings should translate into other areas of research on coalition formation, including government formation by different parties or the electoral bases of party coalitions. In areas where reaching a legitimate group decision is necessary, our results suggest that providing public hearings appears to help decision makers begin the process of forming coalitions while providing a measure of transparency.

Continuing the Conversation on the Great Conversation: Future Research

For all that we believe our analysis has done to inform, we certainly do not think it is—or should be—the last word on the study of oral arguments. Quite the contrary. Our search for the best available data led us to cover multiple Court eras. Chapter 2, which focuses on interruptions, spans several recent terms, while chapters 3 and 4 look at several terms during the early years of the Rehnquist Court. This broad time horizon does much to enhance the generalizability of our results but also leaves us with an unfortunate lack of overlap between raw oral argument materials—that is, the voice-identified transcripts—and the private papers that provide an unparalleled window into the justices' minds and decision-making processes. As earlier transcripts become voice-identified via the Oyez Project, however, this problem will be eliminated, thereby enabling the future pairing of transcript and archival data.

This development, in turn, will open the door to further probing of dynamics on the Court that our analysis cannot address. Consider, for example, variation in how justices behave during oral arguments. As noted earlier, Justice Antonin Scalia is a prolific questioner, while Justice Clarence Thomas is nearly mute. Both Scalia and Thomas—in addition to their seven colleagues—benefit from listening during oral argument. By turning the tables, however, we can pose a distinct question that is, for our money at least, equally interesting: Under what conditions do justices choose to make their positions known during oral arguments? Thomas's relatively extreme preferences and judicial approach put him, according to one study, among the most predictable justices on recent courts (Martin et al. 2004; Ruger et al. 2004). Consequently, there is likely little ambiguity in his colleagues' minds about where he sits in a given case, so Thomas has no incentive to engage in any posturing during oral arguments. We can easily envision a different cost-benefit calculus for justices whose preferences are not as well known (e.g., newly appointed justices) or who lie more toward the Court's ideological middle.

Moving beyond a justice's decision to tip his or her hand, we also see great potential in using these data to examine how the Court moves toward a specific legal rationale in a case. Some evidence suggests that justices use oral argument to raise procedural—as opposed to substantive—issues that might allow them to duck the merits of a case (Johnson and Black 2009). In a similar vein, we might expect to see the justices debating the applicability of competing precedents or whether a case should be decided on statutory or constitutional grounds. Beyond merely having transcripts to document attempts at pushing these points on their colleagues, the private oral argument notes could also be used to assess whether a listening justice found those specific points worth recording.

In the end, our analysis adds to the growing political science literature that demonstrates the importance of the oral arguments for Court decisions. When these data were difficult to obtain (because the audio still resided only in the National Archives on reel-to-reel tapes or on microfiche with non-voice-identified transcripts), scholars provided anecdotal evidence that these proceedings played an integral role in this process (Wasby, D'Amato, and Metrailer 1976). While Johnson (2004) provided strong empirical support, he still focused on fewer than one hundred cases over a fifteen-year span. More recent work provides key systematic evidence that several aspects of oral arguments affect justices' decisions. For example, Johnson, Wahlbeck, and Spriggs (2006) show that the quality of legal arguments corresponds with who wins and loses at the Court. Further, Johnson et al. (2009) find that case outcomes can be predicted based on the number of questions justices raise. In addition, Black et al. (2011) show that the emotions justices reveal with their questions also have predictive power. Our point is simple: In the past decade, it has become clearer than ever that Supreme Court oral arguments can and must be considered an integral part of how justices decide cases. Our findings bolster and extend these previous studies by showing another means by which these proceedings are important for the Court.

But the Supreme Court is only one institution. Even though we provide strong over-time evidence that justices interact with one another as they seek to resolve difficult legal problems, our analysis still has room for extension. There are thirteen circuit courts of appeals, fifty state supreme courts, and countless lower state appellate courts. In addition, other nations have vast numbers of appellate courts. All of these courts have different institutional rules for oral arguments that lead to additional and important questions. For example, how does the length of time devoted to oral argument influence the informational environment? How does the number of judges on the bench change the dialogue and learning environment? And how do different rules for which cases make it to argument affect the impact of these proceedings? To answer these questions, scholars should begin to study this process in lower federal and state courts as well as in courts of other nations and international courts. We leave such analyses for the able hands of future scholars.

Final Thoughts

During a Ninth Circuit judicial conference, Chief Justice John Roberts said, "As a justice, I know how very important oral argument is. As an advocate, I wasn't as sure of this" (qtd. in Garner 2009, 3). Based on the empirical evidence put forth here, we no longer have to take the chief justice's word that oral argument is a very important part of the process—at least for the justices. This book certainly demonstrates the importance of these proceedings, a contribution that has effects for three audiences: scholars of the law and the Supreme Court, attorneys who practice appellate law, and U.S. citizens.

Scholars did not initially give much thought to the importance of oral argument. Very little systematic research was performed on the subject until the late 1990s, and most of this work was generally of a practical nature, providing suggestions for how attorneys could be effective oral advocates. Only recently has the number of social scientific studies of oral argument surged. More important, the scholarly literature has transitioned to a new state of understanding, building a foundation of empirical evidence that suggests that oral arguments matter in ways not previously understood. We expect that as more data become available, scholars will find new insights into the importance of oral argument. The bottom line is that scholars of the Court must now integrate this part of the process into models of decision making.

For attorneys, oral advocacy before the nation's highest court is not an easy task. In fact, many advocates find it an extremely difficult ordeal. Graham (2009) provides one prominent example from Richard Nixon, who complimented the justices after he experienced two arguments before the Court in *Time Inc. v. Hill* (1967). On Chief Justice Earl Warren's last day on the bench, Nixon gave an unprecedented address to the Court, reportedly joking that "the only ordeal more challenging than a presidential press conference was an argument before the Supreme Court" (Graham 2009, 178). This difficulty often stems from the fact that attorneys try to lead the arguments when in fact the justices are leading.

Thus, attorneys who come to the Court with an understanding that their job is not to persuade the justices but to act as an efficient post office for relaying messages back and forth between the justices will likely leave the podium with more satisfaction than frustration. Yogi Berra purportedly once said, "If you ask me anything I don't know, I'm not going to answer." While refusing to respond is not an option for attorneys who practice before the U.S. Supreme Court, it does suggest that if attorneys fail to provide sufficient answers to the questions they are asked, they will hinder the communication between the justices. In other words, this post office function is vital and, if neglected, could stunt or alter the coalition-formation process. But why?

We saw in chapter 3 how Justice Sandra Day O'Connor picked up on the other justices' concerns and interjected her idea for a viable solution to a case, and her solution ended up forming the basis for the majority opinion. But the attorney's response to earlier questions by Byron R. White and John Paul Stevens about state action opened the door for O'Connor to offer her comment. If justices cannot ask questions of the attorneys and instead must rely solely on internal deliberations to resolve a case, they may be less likely to raise such ideas. Oral arguments enable justices to involve attorneys in determining the origin of solutions, and the answers attorneys provide enable justices to feel less constrained as they make decisions.

For citizens, consider the recent Supreme Court confirmation hearings of solicitor general Elena Kagan, where one prominent theme was the possibility of adding cameras to the courtroom. In response to a serious inquiry from Senator Arlen Specter, Kagan's initial response was to deflect the inquiry with humor, remarking that she would have to get her hair done more often. However, she eventually responded that the presence of cameras would be a positive development for the institution and for the American people.[1] While her supporters suggested that Kagan's initial response was an example of her sense of humor, the question implied that American citizens have a serious role to play in democratic governance.

Specifically, the highest court in the land makes decisions on important legal matters that affect all Americans' lives. Yet the public has very little awareness or knowledge of what transpires during the Court's decision-making process (including the only public phase of the process). Consequently, citizens often have difficulty understanding Court decisions beyond the headlines provided in newspapers, on websites, or on television news shows. While opponents of cameras might point to the fact that Americans can easily read the Court's opinions to determine how the law changes, our research suggests that if Americans want to know and understand how the justices make decisions, seeing and hearing the oral arguments is vital.

Readers may remain puzzled about why oral arguments are so helpful and informative to the justices even when attorneys provide poor arguments. The answer helps to bolster our argument in this book. By the justices' own account, these proceedings are the first time they gather to discuss the merits of a case. Justices therefore learn what their colleagues think about a case and its eventual outcome. In a sense, oral argument becomes important despite poor arguments because the nine justices still have to disappear back into the hallways and offices of their marble palace to hammer out a decision and opinion. They know that doing so is a collegial game (see Maltzman, Spriggs, and Wahlbeck 2000) where they need five votes for an opinion to have the full weight of law. Thus, even if the attorneys provide little new information, the justices can still leave oral argument with a good sense of how the case may come down based on their conversation with their colleagues, including the legal grounds on which the decision might be made and how the law might be changed. In short, we know of no other mechanisms in government that take so little time (one hour for each case) yet provide such a remarkable payoff to the American system of government.

Notes

CHAPTER 1

1. To be sure, justices enter oral arguments with a good amount of information about each other's preferences, but legislators and bureaucrats are in the same position before holding hearings on an issue. Moreover, while the justices may have a general idea of each other's preferences, they do not know how each individual colleague will act in a given case because almost every case arrives with a unique fact pattern. Thus, we believe that justices resemble members of Congress or bureaucrats, who often hold hearings before making policy decisions.

2. Segal and Spaeth fail to realize that much of the substantive legal and policy discussion during conference focuses on issues raised at oral arguments even if the words Powell wrote (or his colleagues used) did not include the phrase *oral argument* (see Johnson 2004, 82). In addition, Powell often wrote on his oral argument notes that he found these proceedings helpful. For example, in *United States v. 12 200 Foot Reels of Film* (1973), he wrote, "[A]rgument was helpful, especially as a summary of previous law—read transcript." Again, in *EPA v. Mink* (1973), Powell noted to himself that assistant attorney general Roger C. Cramton provided an "excellent argument (use transcript if I write)."

3. Norms are rules of behavior that are not written but are enforced by groups that interact with one another (see, e.g., Knight 1992). On the Court, a variety of norms structure behavior and interactions among the justices (see, e.g., Epstein, Segal, and Johnson 1996; Epstein and Knight 1998).

4. However, at least one justice discounts this view of oral arguments. When Alito appeared before an audience at Pepperdine Law School, he stated that "oral argument [is not] a conversation among justices through the advocate. That would be a most inefficient method of conveying ideas to one's colleagues" (Stras 2007). Alito's recent actions suggest that he may be revising that view. For example, during the November 2, 2010, oral argument in *Schwarzenegger v. Entertainment Merchants Association,* Alito interrupted the petitioner's attorney, who was responding to a question from Scalia, saying, "Well, I think what Justice Scalia wants to know is what James Madison thought about video games. . . . Did he enjoy them?" This (partly humorous) exchange suggests that Alito acknowledges that he is listening to what information Scalia might want to know. Beyond this example, the preponderance of evidence provided by Johnson (2004) demonstrates that over time and across ideologies, justices believe these proceedings allow them to talk to one another.

5. Previous efforts such as Johnson, Spriggs, and Wahlbeck (2007) certainly address some questions related to those we raise in this book, though they do not specifically emphasize coalition formation.

6. In the past, the justices met on Wednesday and Friday afternoons for conference. During these conferences, they would discuss the merits of cases for which they had heard oral arguments during the same week. In addition, they used part of this time to discuss cases on the "discuss list" (the cases that the Court is considering adding to the agenda) (see, e.g., Caldeira and Wright 1990; Schoen and Wahlbeck 2006). Today, on the Roberts Court, the justices usually meet only on Fridays.

CHAPTER 2

1. To hear the exchange, navigate to http://www.oyez.org/cases/2000-2009/2007/2007_06_8273/argument and click on the purple triangle on the time line.

2. This question is interesting given that this is not how legislatures interact with one another in general debate or in committee hearings. That is, this behavior seems unique to appellate-level judges and justices.

3. Prior to the 2004 term, Supreme Court oral argument transcripts did not provide the name of the justice who was making a comment or asking a question. Rather, all remarks from the justices were denoted by "Question" rather than by a specific justice's name. Beginning in the 2004 term, however, each justice is identified in the transcript. Thus, for the most recent three terms, it is easy to determine who speaks, when, and how often. Thus, we begin with the 2004–7 terms. Between 1998 and 2004, the Oyez Project (www.oyez.org) has provided voice-identified transcripts. Oyez is in the process of using the raw oral argument audio files provided by the National Archives to generate voice-identified transcripts. While voice identification is not yet available prior to 1998, the Oyez Project plans to provide full audio and voice-identified transcripts back to 1955, when the Court began to record all of its oral arguments.

4. We do not directly account for the cases where the Court grants more than one hour (e.g., *Bush v. Gore* [2000]), but even compensating for the few cases with increased time, the justices ask more than one hundred questions per argument.

5. For this reason, many experts on appellate advocacy at the Court warn counsel to not create an oration to present to the Court (see, e.g., Stern et al. 2002). Rather, counsel should have a general argument outline that can be altered based on whether the justices' questions move the argument.

6. One piece of evidence that supports the randomness of any errors associated with our measurement procedure is that if it were biased, we would expect our measures to indicate that chief justices interrupt other justices more often because of structural features associated with the position, which is responsible for keeping oral arguments on schedule (and thus cutting off advocates and justices, occasionally midsentence). For example, during the *Danforth* argument, Breyer was the last speaker during Diamond's session, and Roberts then followed Breyer to recall Butler (attorney for the petitioner) for rebuttal. But even this structural feature does not evidence greater interruptions for either Rehnquist or Roberts (see figure 3). In counting justices' names, we had to account for the fact that during our sample period, Roberts both argued before the Court

and joined the Court. Our computer script differentiates between his appearances in these capacities.

7. Our data include eleven justices, but as is discussed subsequently in greater detail, Clarence Thomas only very rarely speaks during oral argument. As a result, we cannot generate a density plot of the number of times he speaks during oral argument because of the high proportion of zeroes.

8. However, even a slow day for Scalia eclipses the activity of many of his colleagues. His 25th percentile value (roughly eighteen questions) is approximately equal to Rehnquist's median level of questioning and is equivalent to the 75th percentile value for O'Connor. Furthermore, a session of eighteen questions asked by Alito would be deemed an outlier, and Thomas has never had a session in which he asked more than a dozen questions.

9. *FEC v. McConnell* (2003) (119 questions) and *BP America v. Burton* (2006) (102 questions).

10. Doing so is beyond the capacity of this chapter because only two new justices (Alito and Roberts) joined the bench during the terms included in our analysis. Moreover, both were still—by the commonly used metric of two complete terms of service (see, e.g., Maltzman, Spriggs, and Wahlbeck 2000)—freshman justices during the last term of our analysis (2006). Accordingly, we would not be able to make reliable inferences about this hypothesis; as a result, we omit this variable from our model.

11. *Virginia v. Black* (2003) is available at http://www.oyez.org/cases/2000-2009/2002/2002_01_1107.

12. In *Jama v. Immigration and Customs Enforcement* (2004), Souter had the longest utterance (453 words). The tenth-longest speaking turn belongs to Breyer (359 words), in *Muehler v. Mena* (2004). Of the remaining eight utterances, Breyer spoke five and Souter spoke three.

13. Indeed, when justices break the norm of collegiality, they may be admonished. For example, in *U.S. v. R.L.C.* (1991), Rehnquist asked Stevens and Scalia to stop talking so much (see figure 4 for Blackmun's December 10, 1991, oral argument notes, in which he relates this interaction): "CJ mentions JPS & AS are talking too much." To hear the actual exchange (where Rehnquist admonishes Scalia), navigate to http://www.press.umich.edu/titleDetailDesc.do?id=4599894 and click on the link for *R.L.C.* This incident is consistent with the literature discussed in the previous section.

14. The chief did not use the exact phrase ("Shut up") that Blackmun wrote, but his point is the same, especially given the tone of his voice. To hear the exchange, navigate to http://www.press.umich.edu/titleDetailDesc.do?id=4599894 and click on the link for *R.L.C.*

15. Stevens's reputation for being polite may stem from his tendency to ask permission to ask questions during oral argument (see Toobin 2010). For instance, in *Hamdan v. Rumsfeld* (2006), three of his questions began with "May I ask . . ." Usually, as in this case, he only asked permission with his first question but did not do so if he continued with a series of questions.

16. Thomas is just under 6 percent, but because he speaks so rarely during oral argument, we do not draw strong conclusions from this finding.

17. The correlation coefficient is 0.62 with a 95 percent confidence interval of [0.04, 0.89]. This finding means that the relationship is statistically significant at the 95 percent level.

18. To hear this exchange, navigate to http://www.http://www.press.umich.edu/titleDetailDesc.do?id=4599894 and click on the link for *Bush v. Gore* (1).

19. To hear this exchange, navigate to http://www.http://www.press.umich.edu/titleDetailDesc.do?id=4599894 and click on the link for *Bush v. Gore* (2).

20. To hear this exchange, navigate to http://www.http://www.press.umich.edu/titleDetailDesc.do?id=4599894 and click on the link for *Bush v. Gore* (3).

21. To hear this exchange, navigate to http://www.press.umich.edu/titleDetailDesc.do?id=4599894 and click on the link for *McConnell v. FEC* (1).

22. To hear this exchange, navigate to http://www.press.umich.edu/titleDetailDesc.do?id=4599894 and click on the link for *McConnell v. FEC* (2).

23. In a 5-4 opinion written by Kennedy, the Supreme Court upheld Hiibel's conviction because the search, which simply constituted asking Hiibel's name, was minimally intrusive. In short, the majority posited there was no Fifth Amendment violation because Hiibel never justified why giving the officer his name would lead to self-incrimination.

24. To hear this exchange beginning with Justice Ginsburg's question, navigate to http://www.press.umich.edu/titleDetailDesc.do?id=4599894 and click on the link for *Hiibel v. Sixth Judicial District of Nevada.*

25. We expect that if justices want to change the course of the discussion, they are most likely to interrupt a colleague with whom they are most likely to disagree.

26. Indeed, colleagues punish justices who break collegial norms in other venues. Johnson, Spriggs, and Wahlbeck (2005) show that when the chief justice broke the collegial norm of voting during conference, his colleagues would become upset with him and sometimes threatened to exact revenge.

27. More than one justice may try to interrupt a particular speaker at one time (as in the exchange in *Bush v. Gore*). Our coding scheme allows us to capture these possible multiple interruptions. Conversely, we may lose some data because we code only immediate interruptions rather than justices' delayed responses to a particular point. Because our intent is to determine how justices listen to one another and react to specific points, we are comfortable with our coding scheme. In addition, any concerns about listening and then responding to a colleague are captured by our analysis of Blackmun and Powell in the next chapter.

28. In some cases, one of the nine justices may not be present for oral arguments. As a result, not all utterances yield the full eight observations in a case.

29. As a consequence of the dependency inherent to our data (e.g., if Souter interrupts O'Connor, Scalia by definition cannot), we followed the approach taken by the opinion-assignment literature (i.e., Maltzman and Wahlbeck 2004, 555) and initially estimated a random effects logistic regression model. Doing so allows us to estimate the likelihood that a specific justice will interrupt another justice while accounting for the correlation of errors with other justices in the choice set. Results from our random effects model fail to reject the null hypothesis that the true nature of the random effect is zero ($p = 0.47$). This is to say that the model collapses into a standard logistic regression model, which is what we present in table 1. Our results are also the same if we instead estimate a rare events logit model (King and Zeng 2001a, b).

30. A counterpoint is that perhaps justices interrupt ideologically distant foes simply to be argumentative, with no particular goal in mind. We have several reasons to believe that this is not the case. First, with only one hour, the justices have a finite amount

of time in which to gather information and to signal opposing justices. Second, as we demonstrate, interrupting comes with a cost, where being argumentative results in being interrupted more often by others. This, in turn, substantially undercuts the value of a justice's utterances. Finally, while in isolated cases a justice may exemplify obstinate and stubborn behavior, there is no systematic evidence to suggest that justices ask questions with no particular goal in mind.

CHAPTER 3

1. To see all of these notes, organized by docket number within terms, navigate to http://z.umn.edu/trj/ and click on the link to "Harry A. Blackmun and Lewis F. Powell Oral Argument Notes 1970–1994."

2. To hear this clip or the entire argument of *Batson v. Kentucky,* navigate to http://www.press.umich.edu/titleDetailDesc.do?id=4599894 and click on the link for *Batson v. Kentucky* (1).

3. To hear this clip, navigate to http://www.press.umich.edu/titleDetailDesc.do?id=4599894 and click on the link for *Batson v. Kentucky* (2).

4. Powell's oral argument notes also reflect the salience of race in this case. On the third page of his notes, at the top it says "Pearson (Asst AG of KY—a black)," a reference to Rickie L. Pearson, the attorney representing the respondent.

5. To hear this clip, navigate to http://www.press.umich.edu/titleDetailDesc.do?id=4599894 and click on the link for *Batson v. Kentucky* (3).

6. Johnson (2004) argues that because Powell was judicious in what he wrote about his colleagues—only about 10 percent of his notes concern questions or comments they made—scholars can infer that he wrote only about what he deemed key points.

7. We draw these memos from Wahlbeck, Spriggs, and Maltzman (2009).

8. More specifically, the Court remanded the case back to the lower court with instructions to reverse Batson's conviction if the "facts establish, prima facie, purposeful discrimination and the prosecution does not come forward with a neutral explanation for his action" (majority opinion, 100). On remand, approximately two years since the original trial (and more than four years since the original indictment), the prosecutor now faced a difficult task—he had to produce a neutral explanation for his peremptory challenges, which presumably would be based primarily on his memory and notes. At the time, Batson was serving a twenty-year sentence, and with both sides seeking to avoid the risk of a retrial, Batson pled guilty to burglary in exchange for five years in prison (Stewart 2005).

9. In using psychological research on motivated reasoning, Braman (2009) makes an argument that is consistent with ours. Specifically, she argues that judges engage in a biased reasoning process (i.e., motivated reasoning) in which they are unconsciously predisposed "to find authority consistent with their attitudes more convincing than cited authority that goes against desired outcomes" (5). Viewed in this light, justices would be more likely to listen to ideological allies at oral argument.

10. To see these notes, navigate to http://z.umn.edu/trj/ and click on the link to "Harry A. Blackmun and Lewis F. Powell Oral Argument Notes 1970–1994," then select the "1985 Term" notes for Powell. Finally, under Docket 85-1377, click on page 7.

11. Braman (2009) offers an alternative theoretical reason for why ideological foes listen to one another. Specifically, because judges share commonly accepted norms about the importance of accuracy in legal decision making, an ideological foe who makes salient the presence (or absence) of crucial case facts can constrain another justice's ability to embrace ideologically biased arguments. Thus, justices may listen to ideological foes not because the justices are seeking to craft counterarguments but because they are compelled to do so when following the law. While this reasoning seems plausible for lower court judges, where threat of reversal creates a strong incentive to follow case law, it is inconsistent with the evidence we find for oral arguments at the U.S. Supreme Court.

12. To see these notes, navigate to http://z.umn.edu/trj/ and click on the link to "Harry A. Blackmun and Lewis F. Powell Oral Argument Notes 1970–1994," then select the "1971 Term" notes for Blackmun. Finally, click on Docket 71-1017.

13. The accepted form of measuring justices' ideological predilections, Martin-Quinn scores (Martin and Quinn 2002), demonstrates this point. Specifically, for the term in which *Gravel* was decided, Blackmun's Martin-Quinn ideological score was 1.84, which is fairly conservative on a scale where 0 represents exactly moderate. In contrast, Brennan and Douglas were much more liberal, as their scores on the continuum were –1.34 and –6.49, respectively, for this term. To further illustrate the point, Blackmun's Minnesota Twin, Warren Burger, had a conservative Martin-Quinn score of 2.49.

14. Blackmun also noted one of White's questions during oral argument. This point, which we address in our next hypothesis, concerns White's status as the median justice in this case.

15. To see these notes, navigate to http://z.umn.edu/trj/ and click on the link to "Harry A. Blackmun and Lewis F. Powell Oral Argument Notes 1970–1994," then select the "1973 Term" notes for Blackmun. Finally, click on Docket 72-1554.

16. To see these notes, navigate to http://z.umn.edu/trj/ and click on the link to "Harry A. Blackmun and Lewis F. Powell Oral Argument Notes 1970–1994," then select the "1975 Term" notes for Blackmun or Powell. Finally, click on Docket 75-339.

17. To see these notes, navigate to http://z.umn.edu/trj/ and click on the link to "Harry A. Blackmun and Lewis F. Powell Oral Argument Notes 1970–1994," then select the "1973 Term" notes for Powell. Finally, click on Docket 72-1118.

18. To see these notes, navigate to http://z.umn.edu/trj/ and click on the link to "Harry A. Blackmun and Lewis F. Powell Oral Argument Notes 1970–1994," then select the "1976 Term" notes for Blackmun. Finally, click on Docket 76-413.

19. Blackmun usually referred to his colleagues by last initial, with a few exceptions. For example, he always noted himself as *X*. When there were two justices whose names began with *S* (Stewart and Stevens), he called Stevens *V*. Later, when Souter joined the Court, Stevens was *S*, while Souter was *D* (for "David"). Finally, he called Scalia either *A* (for "Antonin") or *N* (for "Nino," his nickname). As chief justice, Rehnquist was *CJ*.

20. His prediction was spot-on in Patterson, with five conservative votes on remand (OR) and four liberal votes in the minority, including himself.

21. The box on the last page of Powell's notes highlights his views on Matson's argument on behalf of the National Organization for Women: "Nothing helpful." This suggests to us that Powell, like Blackmun with his grades, differentiates among the quality of arguments provided by the attorneys. Powell notes that an argument was unhelpful in other cases, including *Maher v. Roe* (1976), where he writes under the appellant's

attorney (Walsh, assistant attorney general of Connecticut), "A third rate argument—of no help whatever. Another example of inadequacy of representation sent up here."

22. Positive contagion is simply the idea that as soon as a recording justice—i.e., Blackmun or Powell—had taken note of an initial comment made by a colleague, his probability of taking a second note is higher. A Poisson regression model assumes that no contagion exists in the data.

23. Our model focuses on including variables motivated by our theory and those that might ostensibly be correlated with our key variables of interest. In other words, we adopt an approach of parsimony over sheer explanatory power. The inclusion of other variables such as issue area dummies and their ilk would likely yield some statistically significant results. However, to the extent that they are unrelated to our key variables, there is no pressing need to include them.

24. In figure 17 (and others that follow), we use separate panels—and scales on the y-axis—to display our results. This presentational decision flows from the fact that while both Blackmun and Powell left evidence of their listening, they employed distinct note-taking processes and recorded comments at different baseline rates. Blackmun, for example, took fewer lines of notes overall than Powell did but had a broader range of references.

25. When Blackmun first joined the Court, he was generally considered a conservative; he subsequently drifted to the left. Hence, colleagues on the bench who at one time would be considered ideologically close would later appear far away. To demonstrate, Blackmun's Martin-Quinn (MQ) score during the 1970 term, his first, was 1.89, which is fairly conservative. However, by the 1985 term, his MQ ideal point was relatively liberal at –0.79, a shift of almost three full units. To put that in perspective, in 1985 O'Connor's MQ score was 1.23 and Rehnquist's MQ score was 3.47; both justices would have been close to Blackmun's in his early court days.

26. Of course, we might not be able to find such a relationship because Powell was the median for a good portion of cases in our sample.

27. The action codes from the Burger Court Opinion Writing Database (Wahlbeck, Spriggs, and Maltzman 2009) associated with each category are as follows: (A) 300, 301, 302, 304; (B) 400, 402, 403; (C) 211, 212, 213, 214, 324, 325, 411, 412, 414, 432, 501, 502; (D) 202, 203, 204, 205. We omitted the following action codes from our dependent variable (i.e., coded as missing values): 220, 221, 222, 223, 303, 320, 321, 322, 323, 330, 410, 420, 440, 441, 442, 460, 500, 510.

28. We do not include the squared value of *Ideological Distance* because while we have a theoretical reason to expect a nonlinear relationship in terms of notation behavior, there is no reason to believe that a justice would most prefer to join an opinion that is "moderately" distant from his or her ideal point.

29. This model requires sustaining an assumption of the independence of irrelevant alternatives (IIA). Broadly speaking, IIA requires that the categories of our dependent variable cannot be deemed as plausible substitutes for one another. Given the clear substantive differences across the categories, we believe that this assumption is plausible.

While some scholars deploy the Hausman-McFadden or Small-Hsaio tests to assess IIA, we follow the advice of Long and Freese (2006, 243–44): Citing a long list of simulation studies, they counsel specifically against relying on these tests.

30. Interpreting figures 23 and 24 requires focusing on the size of each shaded region for the relevant number of references made to each colleague displayed on the

x-axis. We generated these values using the SPost series of commands as implemented in Stata 11 by Long and Freese (2006).

CHAPTER 4

1. Blackmun's convention was to use a plus sign as shorthand for affirming a lower-court decision and a minus sign as shorthand for reversing a lower-court decision.

2. To hear this clip or the entire argument of *Cruzan v. Missouri,* navigate to http://www.press.umich.edu/titleDetailDesc.do?id=4599894 and click on the link for *Cruzan v. Missouri Dept. of Health.*

3. We operationalize this point as the total number of lines he wrote in his notes. This is a reasonable argument since the length of his notes indicates his assessment of the relevance of the arguments from the attorneys and from his colleagues.

4. The question mark was Blackmun's way of noting that he was not clear about a colleague's vote.

5. If the chief justice is in the majority coalition at the time of the conference, he has the prerogative of assigning a justice to write the majority opinion (and can choose himself).

6. For another example where Blackmun predicted every vote correctly, see *Board of Education of Oklahoma City v. Dowell* (1991). He did, however, initially express uncertainty about White before correctly predicting his vote. To see the notes in this case, navigate to http://z.umn.edu/trj/ and click on the link to "Harry A. Blackmun and Lewis F. Powell Oral Argument Notes 1970–1994," then select the "1990 Term" notes for Blackmun. Finally, click on Docket 89-1080.

7. *Tower v. Glover* originated when Billy Irl Glover was arrested on robbery charges and subsequently convicted at trial in Oregon. He later filed and lost an appeal in state court. Glover also filed an action in federal court alleging that Bruce Tower and Gary Babcock, his public defenders at trial and on appeal, respectively, conspired with state officials to secure his conviction. The U.S. District Court dismissed the action, citing precedent that suggested that public defenders were absolutely immune from suits of this nature. The Ninth Circuit later reversed the District Court's decision, citing different precedent. The Supreme Court was left with the question of whether public defenders were immune from liability for intentional misconduct. The Supreme Court ultimately affirmed the Ninth Circuit and ruled that state public defenders are not immune from liability for conspiring with state officials to deny a plaintiff's constitutional rights.

8. The four justices with question marks next to their names were O'Connor, Souter, Stevens, and Scalia. His prediction regarding White was wrong even though Blackmun thought he was certain about how White would act. To see his notes in this case, navigate to http://z.umn.edu/trj/ and click on the link to "Harry A. Blackmun and Lewis F. Powell Oral Argument Notes 1970–1994," then select the "1990 Term" notes for Blackmun. Finally, click on Docket 90-26.

9. To see these notes, navigate to http://z.umn.edu/trj/ and click on the link to "Harry A. Blackmun and Lewis F. Powell Oral Argument Notes 1970–1994." For *Zbaraz,* select the "1979 Term" notes for Blackmun and select Docket 79-4. For *Barry,* select the "1991 Term" notes for Blackmun and click on Docket 90-7477.

10. This hypothesis may seem counterintuitive. However, because the median is so central to coalition formation (as the literature indicates), the median is also one of the most closely watched justices. Therefore, we expect Blackmun to be more likely to predict the median's vote.

11. We are careful to distinguish between motives and behavior. Indeed, it is entirely possible that Blackmun may want to make a prediction in a complex case but because of the number of issues with which he must deal, he is less likely to do so.

12. The Sartori selection model is closely related to the commonly employed Heckman probit model but does not require the existence of an exclusionary variable (i.e., an instrument that is highly correlated with the selection stage but entirely uncorrelated with the outcome stage).

13. We have also examined whether Blackmun was simply more successful at predicting some of his colleagues' votes than others. As a general matter, the data do not suggest the presence of any so-called justice effects. An exception to this statement was Blackmun's uncanny ability to predict how Souter would vote. Blackmun was successful in fifteen of the sixteen cases where he attempted to predict Souter's vote, an accuracy rate of roughly 94 percent. Despite the small number of observations, this rate is systematically higher than his success rate for any other justice. For more information, see figure 34.

CHAPTER 5

1. Ironically, Kagan's nomination came on the heels of the retirement of David Souter, who once opined that cameras would be allowed in the Supreme Court when they rolled in over his dead body.

References

Albarracin, Dolores. 2002. "Cognition in Persuasion: An Analysis of Information Processing in Response to Persuasive Communication." *Advances in Experimental Social Psychology* 34:61–130.

Bettenhausen, Kenneth, and J. Keith Murnighan. 1985. "The Emergence of Norms in Competitive Decision-Making Groups." *Administrative Science Quarterly* 30 (3): 350–72.

Biskupic, Joan. 2006. "Justices Make Points by Questioning Lawyers." *USA Today,* October 5. Available at http://www.usatoday.com/news/washington/judicial/2006-10-05-oral-arguments_x.htm. Accessed September 27, 2010.

Black, Ryan C., and Ryan J. Owens. 2009. "Agenda Setting in the Supreme Court: The Collision of Policy and Jurisprudence." *Journal of Politics* 71 (3): 1062–75.

Black, Ryan C., Sarah A. Treul, Timothy R. Johnson, and Jerry Goldman. 2011. "Emotions, Oral Arguments, and Supreme Court Decision Making." *Journal of Politics* 73 (2): 572–81.

Bonneau, Chris W., Thomas H. Hammond, Forrest Maltzman, and Paul J. Wahlbeck. 2007. "Agenda Control, the Median Justice, and the Majority Opinion on the U.S. Supreme Court." *American Journal of Political Science* 51 (4): 890–905.

Boucher, Robert L., Jr., and Jeffrey A. Segal. 1995. "Supreme Court Justices as Strategic Decision Makers: Aggressive Grants and Defensive Denials on the Vinson Court." *Journal of Politics* 57 (3): 824–37.

Braman, Eileen. 2009. *Law, Politics, and Perception: How Policy Preferences Influence Legal Reasoning.* Charlottesville: University of Virginia Press.

Brandt, Patrick T., and Christina J. Schneider. 2007. "So the Reviewer Told You to Use a Selection Model? Selection Models and the Study of International Relations." Available at polisci2.ucsd.edu/cjschneider/working_papers/pdf/Selection-W041.pdf. Accessed August 29, 2011.

Caldeira, Gregory A., and John R. Wright. 1990. "The Discuss List: Agenda Building in the Supreme Court." *Law and Society Review* 24 (3): 807–36.

Caldeira, Gregory A., John R. Wright, and Christopher J. W. Zorn. 1999. "Sophisticated Voting and Gate-Keeping in the Supreme Court." *Journal of Law, Economics, and Organization* 15 (3): 549–72.

Carroll, Jennifer S. 2000. "Appellate Specialization and the Art of Appellate Advocacy." *Florida Bar Journal* 74 (June): 107–9.

Carrubba, Clifford, Barry Friedman, Andrew D. Martin, and Georg Vanberg. 2007.

"Does the Median Justice Control the Content of Supreme Court Opinions?" Paper presented at the Annual Conference on Empirical Legal Studies.

Collins, Paul M., Jr. 2008a. "Amici Curiae and Dissensus on the U.S. Supreme Court." *Journal of Empirical Legal Studies* 5 (1): 143–70.

Collins, Paul M., Jr. 2008b. *Friends of the Court: Interest Groups and Judicial Decision Making.* New York: Oxford University Press.

Corley, Pamela C. 2008. "The Supreme Court and Opinion Content: The Influence of Parties' Briefs." *Political Research Quarterly* 61 (3): 468–78.

Cowana, Robin, and Nicolas Jonard. 2004. "Network Structure and the Diffusion of Knowledge." *Journal of Economic Dynamics and Control* 28 (12):1557–75.

Crawford, Vincent P., and Joel Sobel. 1982. "Strategic Information Transmission." *Econometrica* 50 (6): 1431–51.

C-SPAN. 2009. *The Supreme Court: Home to America's Highest Court.* Video. Available at http://supremecourt.c-span.org/Video/TVPrograms/SC_Week_Documentary.aspx. Accessed September 27, 2010.

Denniston, Lyle. 2007. "Commentary: What Does the Supreme Court Really Do? (SCOTUS-blogpost)." Available at http://www.scotusblog.com/2007/10/commentary-what-does-the-supreme-court-really-do/. Accessed September 27, 2010.

Downs, Anthony. 1957. *An Economic Theory of Democracy.* New York: Harper.

Easton, David A. 1953. *The Political System: An Inquiry into the State of Political Science.* New York: Knopf.

Epstein, Lee, and Jack Knight. 1998. *The Choices Justices Make.* Washington, DC: CQ Press.

Epstein, Lee, Jeffrey A. Segal, and Timothy Johnson. 1996. "The Claim of Issue Creation on the U.S. Supreme Court." *American Political Science Review* 90 (4): 845–52.

Farrell, Joseph, and Matthew Rabin. 1996. "Cheap Talk." *Journal of Economic Perspectives* 10 (3): 103–18.

Feldman, M. 1994. *The Geography of Innovation.* Dordrecht, Netherlands: Kluwer Academic.

Frederick, David C. 2003. *Supreme Court and Appellate Advocacy.* St. Paul, MN: Thomson/West.

Freedman, David A., and Jasjeet S. Sekhon. 2010. "Endogeneity in Probit Response Models." *Political Analysis* 18 (2): 138–50.

Gamson, William A. 1961. "A Theory of Coalition Formation." *American Sociological Review* 26 (3): 373–82.

Garner, Bryan A. 2009. *The Winning Oral Argument: Enduring Principles with Supporting Comments from the Literature.* 2nd ed. St. Paul, MN: Thomson/West.

Graham, Fred. 2009. "*Time Inc. v. Hill:* A Future President Makes His Case." In *A Good Quarrel: America's Top Legal Reporters Share Stories from Inside the Supreme Court,* ed. Timothy R. Johnson and Jerry Goldman, 169–78. Ann Arbor: University of Michigan Press.

Greenhouse, Linda. 1989. "Oblique Clash between 2 Justices Mirrors Tensions about Abortion." *New York Times,* November 30. Available at http://www.nytimes.com/1989/11/30/us/oblique-clash-between-2-justices-mirrors-tensions-about-abortion.html. Accessed September 27, 2010.

Greenhouse, Linda. 1993. "Justices Spar over Validity of a District Based on Race." *New York Times,* April 21.

Hagle, Timothy M. 1993a. "'Freshman Effects' for Supreme Court Justices." *American Journal of Political Science* 37 (4): 1142–57.

Hagle, Timothy M. 1993b. "Strategic Retirements: A Political Model of Turnover on the United States Supreme Court." *Political Behavior* 15 (1): 25–48.

Hammond, Thomas H., Chris W. Bonneau, and Reginald S. Sheehan. 2005. *Strategic Behavior and Policy Choice on the U.S. Supreme Court.* Stanford: Stanford University Press.

Harvey, Anna L., and Barry Friedman. 2006. "Pulling Punches: Congressional Constraint on the Supreme Court's Constitutional Rulings, 1987–2000." *Legislative Studies Quarterly* 31 (4): 533–62.

Hughes, Charles Evans. 1928. *The Supreme Court of the United States.* New York: Columbia University Press.

Jaffe, A., M. Trajtenberg, and R. Henderson. 1993. "Geographic Localization of Knowledge Spillovers as Evidenced by Patent Citations." *Quarterly Journal of Economics* 108 (3): 577–98.

Johnson, Timothy R. 2004. *Oral Arguments and Decision Making on the United States Supreme Court.* Albany: State University of New York Press.

Johnson, Timothy R., and Ryan C. Black. 2009. "Supreme Court Oral Arguments as a Heresthetical Tool: Threshold Questions from the Bench." Paper presented at the Southern Political Science Association.

Johnson, Timothy R., Ryan C. Black, Jerry Goldman, and Sarah A. Treul. 2009. "Inquiring Minds Want to Know: Do Justices Tip Their Hands with Their Questions at Oral Arguments in the U.S. Supreme Court?" *Washington University Journal of Law and Policy* 29 (1): 241–61.

Johnson, Timothy R., James F. Spriggs II, and Paul J. Wahlbeck. 2005. "Passing and Strategic Voting on the U.S. Supreme Court." *Law and Society Review* 39 (2): 349–77.

Johnson, Timothy R., James F. Spriggs II, and Paul J. Wahlbeck. 2007. "Supreme Court Oral Advocacy: Does It Affect the Justices' Decisions?" *Washington University Law Review* 85 (3): 457–527.

Johnson, Timothy R., Paul J. Wahlbeck, and James F. Spriggs II. 2006. "The Evaluation of Oral Argumentation before the U.S. Supreme Court." *American Political Science Review* 100 (1): 99–113.

Kahan, James P., and Amnon Rapoport. 1984. *Theories of Coalition Formation.* Hillsdale, NJ: Erlbaum.

Kanki, Barbara, V. G. Folk, and C. M. Irwin. 1991. "Communication Variations and Aircrew Communication Variations and Aircrew Performance." *International Journal of Aviation Psychology* 1 (2): 149–62.

Kaufman, Irving R. 1978. "Appellate Advocacy in the Federal Courts." *Federal Rules Decisions* 79:165–72.

King, Gary, and Langche Zeng. 2001a. "Explaining Rare Events in International Relations." *International Organization* 55 (3): 693–715.

King, Gary, and Langche Zeng. 2001b. "Logistic Regression in Rare Events Data." *Political Analysis* 9 (2): 137–63.

Knight, Jack. 1992. *Institutions and Social Conflict.* Cambridge: Cambridge University Press.

Kollock, Peter, Phillip Blumstein, and Pepper Schwartz. 1985. "Sex and Power in Interaction." *American Sociological Review* 50 (1): 34–47.

Liptak, Adam. 2010. "No Vote-Trading Here." *New York Times,* May 14. Available at http://www.nytimes.com/2010/05/16/weekinreview/16liptak.html. Accessed September 27, 2010.

Long, J. Scott. 1997. *Regression Models for Categorical and Limited Dependent Variables.* Thousand Oaks, CA: Sage.

Long, J. Scott, and Jeremy Freese. 2006. *Regression Models for Categorical Dependent Variables Using Stata.* 2nd ed. College Station, TX: Stata.

Lowy, Joan. 2009. "Court to Weigh State's Duty to English Learners." *Associated Press,* April 20. Available at http://seattletimes.nwsource.com/html/politics/2009086744_apscotusenglishlearners.html. Accessed September 27, 2010.

Lupia, Arthur, and Mathew D. McCubbins. 1998. *The Democratic Dilemma: Can Citizens Learn What They Need to Know?* New York: Cambridge University Press.

Maltzman, Forrest, James F. Spriggs II, and Paul J. Wahlbeck. 2000. *Crafting Law on the Supreme Court: The Collegial Game.* New York: Cambridge University Press.

Maltzman, Forrest, and Paul J. Wahlbeck. 2004. "A Conditional Model of Opinion Assignment on the Supreme Court." *Political Research Quarterly* 57 (4): 551–63.

Martin, Andrew D., and Kevin M. Quinn. 2002. "Dynamic Ideal Point Estimation via Markov Chain Monte Carlo for the U.S. Supreme Court, 1953–1999." *Political Analysis* 10 (2): 134–53.

Martin, Andrew D., Kevin M. Quinn, Theodore W. Ruger, and Pauline T. Kim. 2004. "Competing Approaches to Predicting Supreme Court Decision Making." *Perspectives on Politics* 2 (4): 761–67.

Morrow, James D. 1994. *Game Theory for Political Scientists.* Princeton: Princeton University Press.

Murnighan, J. Keith, and Eugene Szwajkowski. 1979. "Coalition Bargaining in Four Games That Include a Veto Player." *Journal of Personality and Social Psychology* 37 (11): 1933–46.

Murphy, Walter F. 1964. *Elements of Judicial Strategy.* Chicago: University of Chicago Press.

Nicholson, Chris, and Paul M. Collins Jr. 2008. "The Solicitor General's Amicus Curiae Strategies in the Supreme Court." *American Politics Research* 36 (3): 382–415.

O'Brien, David M. 2000. *Storm Center: The Supreme Court in American Politics.* 5th ed. New York: Norton.

PBS. 1988. *This Honorable Court.* Video. Alexandria, VA: PBS Video.

Prevezer, M., and P. Swann. 1996. "A Comparison of the Dynamics of Industrial Clustering in Computing and Biotechnology." *Research Policy* 25 (7): 1139–57.

Reeves, Jay. 2009. "Clarence Thomas to Other Supreme Court Justices: Be Quiet." *Huffington Post,* October 23. Available at http://www.huffingtonpost.com/2009/10/24/clarence-thomas-to-other-_n_332464.html. Accessed July 8, 2010.

Rehnquist, William H. 2001. *The Supreme Court.* Rev. and updated ed. New York: Vintage.

Riker, William H. 1962. *The Theory of Political Coalitions.* New Haven: Yale University Press.

Roberts, John G. 2005. "Testimony before the Senate Judiciary Committee." *New York Times,* September 13. Available at http://www.nytimes.com/2005/09/13/politics/politicsspecial1/13text-roberts.html. Accessed September 17, 2006.

Robinette, John J. 1975. "A Counsel Looks at the Court." *Canadian Bar Review* 53 (3): 558–62.

Rohde, David W., and Harold J. Spaeth. 1976. *Supreme Court Decision-Making.* San Francisco: Freeman.

Ruger, Theodore W., Pauline T. Kim, Andrew D. Martin, and Kevin M. Quinn. 2004. "The Supreme Court Forecasting Project: Legal and Political Science Approaches to Predicting Supreme Court Decisionmaking." *Columbia Law Review* 104 (4): 1150–1209.

Sartori, Anne E. 2003. "An Estimator for Some Binary-Outcome Selection Models without Exclusion Restrictions." *Political Analysis* 11 (2): 111–38.

Schlager, Edella. 1995. "Policy Making and Collective Action: Defining Coalitions within the Advocacy Coalition Framework." *Policy Sciences* 28 (3): 243–70.

Schoen, Ryan, and Paul J. Wahlbeck. 2006. "The Discuss List and Agenda-Setting on the Supreme Court." Paper presented at the Southern Political Science Association.

Segal, Jeffrey A., and Harold J. Spaeth. 2002. *The Supreme Court and the Attitudinal Model Revisited.* New York: Cambridge University Press.

Shapiro, Stephen M. 1984. "Symposium on Supreme Court Advocacy: Oral Argument in the Supreme Court of the United States." *Catholic University Law Review* 33 (Spring): 529–53.

Sherman, Mark. 2008. "Justice Thomas Silent through More Than Two Years of Supreme Court Arguments." *Law.com,* February 25. Available at http://www.law.com/jsp/article.jsp?id=1203939949026. Accessed February 6, 2009.

Shullman, Sarah Levien. 2004. "The Illusion of Devil's Advocacy: How the Justices of the Supreme Court Foreshadow Their Decisions during Oral Argument." *Journal of Appellate Practice and Process* 6 (2): 271–93.

Smith-Lovin, Lynn, and Charles Brody. 1989. "Interruptions in Group Discussions: The Effects of Gender and Group Composition." *American Sociological Review* 54 (3): 424–35.

Soh, Leen-Kiat, and Costas Tsatsoulis. 2002. "Satisficing Coalition Formation among Agents." In *Proceedings of the First International Joint Conference on Autonomous Agents and Multiagent Systems,* 1062–63. Autonomous Agents Conference, July 15–19, Bologna, Italy.

Solowiej, Lisa, and Thomas L. Brunell. 2003. "The Entrance of Women to the U.S. Congress: The Widow Effect." *Political Research Quarterly* 56 (3): 283–92.

Spriggs, James F., II, Forrest Maltzman, and Paul J. Wahlbeck. 1999. "Bargaining on the U.S. Supreme Court: Justices' Responses to Majority Opinion Drafts." *Journal of Politics* 61 (2): 485–506.

Stern, Robert L., Eugene Gressman, Stephen M. Shapiro, and Kenneth S. Geller. 2002. *Supreme Court Practice.* 8th ed. Washington, DC: Bureau of National Affairs.

Stewart, Kay. 2005. "'Good' Reversal Followed 'Unfair' Trial." Courier-Journal.com. November 6. Accessed February 6, 2012.

Stras, David. 2007. "The Pepperdine Event with Justice Alito and Carter Phillips (SCOTUS-blogpost)." Available at http://www.scotusblog.com/blog/2007/08/09/the-pepperdine-event-with-justice-alito-and-carter-phillips/. Accessed September 27, 2010.

Strodtbeck, Fred L. 1954. "The Family as a Three-Person Group." *American Sociological Review* 19 (1): 23–29.

Strum, Philippa. 2000. "Essay: Change and Continuity on the Supreme Court: Conversations with Justice Harry A. Blackmun." *University of Richmond Law Review* 34 (1): 285–304.

Tarpley, Joan. 2001. "A Comment on Justice O'Connor's Quest for Power and Its Impact on African American Wealth." *South Carolina Law Review* 53 (1): 117–250.

Toobin, Jeffrey. 2007. *The Nine: Inside the Secret World of the Supreme Court.* New York: Doubleday.

Toobin, Jeffrey. 2010. "After Stevens: What Will the Supreme Court Be Like without Its Liberal Leader?" *New Yorker,* March 22.

Totenberg, Nina. 2006. "Roberts' Court Produces More Unanimous Decisions." National Public Radio, May 22. Available at http://www.npr.org/templates/story/story.php?storyId=5421326. Accessed February 6, 2009.

van der Kleij, Rick, Jan Maarten Schraagen, Peter Werkhoven, and Carsten K. W. De Dreu. 2009. "How Conversations Change over Time in Face-to-Face and Video-Mediated Communication." *Small Group Research* 40 (4): 355–81.

von Neumann, John, and Oskar Morgenstern. 1953. *Theory of Games and Economic Behavior.* 3rd ed. Princeton: Princeton University Press.

Wahlbeck, Paul J. 2006. "Strategy and Constraints on Supreme Court Opinion Assignment." *University of Pennsylvania Law Review* 154 (6): 1729–55.

Wahlbeck, Paul J., James F. Spriggs II, and Forrest Maltzman. 1998. "Marshaling the Court: Bargaining and Accommodation on the United States Supreme Court." *American Journal of Political Science* 42 (1): 294–315.

Wahlbeck, Paul J., James F. Spriggs II, and Forrest Maltzman. 2009. "The Burger Court Opinion Writing Database." First Release. Data file and codebook, August 6. Available at http://home.gwu.edu/~wahlbeck/Personal_Homepage/The_Burger_Court_Opinion_Writing_Database.html. Accessed August 29, 2011.

Wasby, Stephen L., Anthony A. D'Amato, and Rosemary Metrailer. 1976. "The Functions of Oral Arguments in the U.S. Supreme Court." *Quarterly Journal of Speech* 62 (4): 410–22.

Wasby, Stephen L., Anthony A. D'Amato, and Rosemary Metrailer. 1977. *Desegregation from Brown to Alexander: An Exploration of Court Strategies.* Carbondale: Southern Illinois University Press.

Wedeking, Justin. 2010. "Supreme Court Litigants and Strategic Framing." *American Journal of Political Science* 54 (3): 617–31.

West, Candace. 1979. "Against Our Will: Male Interruptions of Females in Cross-Sex Conversation." *Annals of New York Academy of Sciences* 327 (June): 81–96.

Wrightsman, Lawrence S. 2008. *Oral Arguments before the Supreme Court: An Empirical Approach.* New York: Oxford University Press.

Index

Note: Page numbers in italics indicate figures.